# THE HIDDEN VICTIMS OF ALZHEIMER'S DISEASE

# THE HIDDEN VICTIMS OF ALZHEIMER'S DISEASE:
## Families Under Stress

Steven H. Zarit
Nancy K. Orr
Judy M. Zarit

NEW YORK UNIVERSITY PRESS
New York & London
1985

Library of Congress Cataloging in Publication Data

Zarit, Steven H.
  The hidden victims of Alzheimer's disease.

  Bibliography: p.
  Includes index.
  1. Alzheimer's disease—Patients—Family relationships.
2. Stress (Psychology)  3. Alzheimer's disease—Patients—
Services for.  I. Orr, Nancy K.  II. Zarit, Judy M.
III. Title.  IV. Title: Families under stress.
[DNLM: 1. Alzhemer's Disease.  Community Health
Services.  3. Counseling.  4. Family.  5. Home Nursing.
WM 220 Z37c]
RC523.Z37  1985      362.1'9683      85–3049
ISBN 0–8147–9662–1
ISBN 0–8147–9663–x (pbk.)

Clothbound editions of New York University Press books are Smyth-
sewn and printed on permanent and durable acid-free paper.

Book design by Ken Venezio

# CONTENTS

# ACKNOWLEDGMENTS

The first drafts of this book were made possible through a grant from the UCLA/USC Long-term Care Gerontology Center. We wish to thank Jon Pynoos and Jody Cohn for their initial support of this project and their encouragement throughout. Support was also provided in part by a grant from the Center for the Studies of the Mental Health of the Aging, National Institute of Mental Health (MH-34507). The clinical work on which this book is based has been carried out at the Andrus Older Adult Center. The Andrus Older Adult Center is a service and training clinic sponsored by the Andrus Gerontology Center of the University of Southern California.

Among the staff and trainees who contributed to the clinical work reflected in this volume, we especially want to note Mary Boutselis, Marla Hassinger, and Joyce Kuppinger for the many ideas and examples which they provided. Additional case material was provided by Terri McWilliams and Shari Miura. Richard Heinrich and Brad Williams were valuable consultants on several cases. Karen Reever, now with the Philadelphia Geriatric Center, was a key person when we were first beginning to work with caregivers, and helped get us on the right track.

For the past five years, the Andrus Older Adult Center has been housed at the St. Vincent Medical Center in Los Angeles. We wish to thank the St. Vincent Medical Center for their generous support and encouragement during that period, and to give special thanks to Sister Francis Sullivan, their Community Health and Education Coordinator. We also want to thank Community Hospital of San Gabriel and Valley Vista Hospital for their generous donation of space for the past two years, which enabled us to develop a satellite program, the Center for Adult Development, in the San Gabriel Valley.

## ACKNOWLEDGMENTS

Our program has been sustained in part by the Andrus Gerontology Center and the Golden Era Associates. We wish especially to acknowledge the support given by Drs. James E. Birren, Dean of the Andrus Center, and David Peterson, Director of the Leonard Davis School of Gerontology.

We are grateful for the suggestions and criticisms made by Sylvia Fox, Kathleen Kelly, Bob Knight, Barbara Mowry, Alan Robbins, Hortense Tingstad, and Claire Weiner, who reviewed an earlier version of this manuscript. May Ng was always patient and helpful in the production of the manuscript.

# THE HIDDEN VICTIMS OF ALZHEIMER'S DISEASE

# CHAPTER 1

# POSITIVE PSYCHOSOCIAL APPROACHES TO DEMENTIA

The dementias are the most devastating and dreaded disorders of later life. Once thought to be an inevitable part of the aging process, dementia is now known to be caused by illnesses such as Alzheimer's disease, which afflict only 5 to 7 percent of the population over age 65 (Mortimer, Schuman & French, 1981). The dementias are characterized by steadily deteriorating memory. At first the loss is minimal and barely distinguishable from the forgetfulness that everyone experiences. Over time, memory loss increases, often accompanied by changes in personality and a loss in the ability to perform daily tasks, such as dressing, bathing, or eating.

The patient is not the only victim of this disease. There are probably no other diseases that involve families so much or have such devastating effects. Even though basic research on the dementias has been increased dramatically in the last ten years, causes are still unknown and there are no effective medical cures. While the search for medical interventions is important, there is also a role for health-care and social-service professionals to improve the quality of care the dementia patient receives and to prevent the burden on families from becoming overwhelming. The approach taken toward an illness can determine whether and how it is treated. If dementia is seen as a chronic, degenerative disease for which there is no known treatment, then the logical conclusion is that nothing can be done. But if the illness is viewed as a problem with many components, some of which can be solved while others cannot, it becomes reasonable to plan interventions. The psychologist, Robert L. Kahn, has described dementia as a "bio-psycho-social phenomenon," and while the biological aspects are not currently treatable as has been indicated, the psychological and social are often amenable to intervention (Kahn, 1975). For example, a common problem reported by families is that the dementia patient misplaces things and then blames others for stealing them. Viewed as a medical problem, the most likely treatment is to prescribe tranquilizing drugs. But these drugs often have undesirable side effects and may even intensify the problem they were meant to ameliorate. The psychosocial approach to intervention would involve exploring possible reasons for the behavior, and examining how the family handles the problem. The following example illustrates this problem.

Mr. Pine cared for his wife, who had shown dementia symptoms for six years. One of the problems that bothered him most was that she accused him of stealing money from her purse, which he was not doing. When this happened, he would try to reason with her, but she would argue, insisting that he had taken it. The situation would escalate until he was shouting at her and she was crying. With the help of a counselor, he was able to understand that her accusations might be a way for her to cover up her memory loss, and that arguing only upset both of them. Instead of arguing, he learned to respond to her accusations by acknowledging she was upset but not trying to reason with her. He would say, "I'm sorry you're upset about your money. Is there anything I can do?" This calmed her down.

## OBJECTIVES OF THIS BOOK

This book has been written primarily for practitioners working in community settings with patients with dementing illnesses or their families. It has been designed both for the generalist, working in a nutrition site or senior multipurpose center, and for the specialist, including social workers, nurses, psychologists and gerontologists, who provide health-related or mental-health services. The book may also serve as an introduction for students interested in problems of aging and dementia, and for family

**FIGURE 1.1.**

Goals for Service Providers

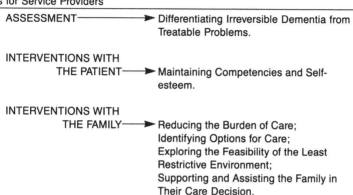

ASSESSMENT ⟶ Differentiating Irreversible Dementia from Treatable Problems.

INTERVENTIONS WITH
THE PATIENT ⟶ Maintaining Competencies and Self-esteem.

INTERVENTIONS WITH
THE FAMILY ⟶ Reducing the Burden of Care;
Identifying Options for Care;
Exploring the Feasibility of the Least Restrictive Environment;
Supporting and Assisting the Family in Their Care Decision.

members working with organizations devoted to Alzheimer's disease. The book gives a framework for understanding dementing illnesses, such as Alzheimer's disease. It examines the causes of memory loss and the symptoms of dementia, provides guidelines for assessment, and describes possible intervention to assist patients and their families (see Figure 1.1).

The first step for those who deal with Alzheimer's disease is to understand what dementia is and how to recognize it. There has always been a tendency to overdiagnose "senility" among older persons, and until recently senility was considered an inevitable consequence of aging. It is now known that the severe memory loss that was formerly called senility is actually a symptom caused by any of several diseases. But because of a lack of knowledge about these diseases, the practice of imprecise diagnosis of dementia has persisted. For example, a recent article in the *Journal of the American Medical Association* found that 26 out of 136 nursing home patients with a diagnosis of senile dementia actually had treatable problems (Sabin, Vitug, & Mark, 1982). Some syndromes which resemble dementia including depression, delirium, nonprogressive brain injuries, as well as changes associated with normal aging, have very different implications for the patients. A delirium and depression are usually treatable while deficits associated with head trauma and normal aging are

3

likely to be fairly stable over time. By learning how to recognize these problems and distinguish them from an irreversible dementia, the individual who is responsible for diagnosing Alzheimer's disease reduces the number of persons who are improperly diagnosed.

If a patient is properly diagnosed as having dementia, well-planned treatment can help the afflicted person function as well as possible. Treatment can maintain the patient's level of competency, boost morale, and minimize behavior problems. Yet probably the most effective and practical measures that can be taken are those which reduce the stress on family members, on whom much of the burden of care falls. Two effective ways of lowering the stress on those who are responsible for providing care are to improve their skills in managing problem behavior and to increase the social support they receive from others. Means for stress management have been developed to aid those who are primarily responsible for providing care. Stress management procedures and their applications in counseling, family meetings, and support groups are described in subsequent chapters.

## Community Care: Why Nursing Homes Are Not the Only Answer

Many professionals, including physicians, social workers, and psychologists, believe that dementia patients cannot be cared for outside of an institutional setting. Some maintain that it is only the guilt of family members that prevents proper placement of all dementia patients in institutions. Oftentimes these professionals try to alleviate the family's guilt to allow them to place their relative in a nursing home. Others believe it is too stressful for family members to provide care, or assume that the patient will become violent or disruptive. Neither of these instances will necessarily happen. This book was written specifically to challenge these beliefs. Families come with many interrelationships and structures. Thus some would not oppose institutionalization as the best care for a loved one. But many others prefer and are quite capable of caring for their impaired relative at home. The

4

goal of advisors to different families therefore must be first to provide knowledge of all options available, second, to explore the feasibility of the least restrictive environment for the dementia patient, and third, to support and assist the family in whatever decision they make.

There are several reasons for viewing nursing-home placement as one option that must be considered in the light of several possible alternatives. First, many families want to provide home care for as long as possible. Even when a family initially requests help in finding a nursing home, it is sometimes the result of a lack of information about alternative forms of care, or their physician or friends have told them to find a nursing home. As a first step it is important to find out why the family is thinking institutionalization and to ask what other alternatives they have tried or considered, including providing care at home. In our experience, the first choice of most families is to keep the dementia patient at home.

One reason given for recommending nursing-home placement is to reduce the burden on the responsible family. However, this approach ignores other kinds of outside help, such as the possibility of community interventions. Moreover, nursing-home placement only shifts the burden families experience, rather than relieving it. The family members will continue to have to visit their relative in the nursing home, and to deal with staff and doctors to try to assure the best care available. Seeing their relative in an institution is in itself stressful, and the family has less control over care with nursing homes than in their own home. Finally, since there is only limited third party payment for nursing home care, placement can be devastating financially, placing even more stress on the family.

Avoiding institutionalization is also much better for the patient's morale. Relocation to a nursing home is a traumatic event for any older person, but can be even more catastrophic for dementia patients. Because of their cognitive deficits, dementia patients have considerable difficulty learning the routines in a nursing home, or even finding their way around. They often panic in their new environment, or create other problems which try the staff's patience, such as wandering or wanting to stay awake at night. While some facilities can manage these problems, many others resort to extreme measures, including the use of high dosages of tranquilizing drugs and restraints to control the patient. Medications often exacerbate rather than alleviate behavior problems. The bizarre behavior of patients in many nursing homes, including hallucinations, restlessness, agitation and motor difficulties, are typical reactions to high doses of medicine. This behavior usually is not observed at home if low- or drug-free regimens are relied upon.

The prevention or delay in putting a dementia patient in a nursing home is a realistic possibility for many families. Some surveys have shown that older people with dementia who are maintained at homes have impairments as severe as those who are in nursing homes. According to one study, the major reason family members place a relative in a nursing home is that the family has become physically, financially, or emotionally exhausted providing care, not because the patient's problems have worsened (Lowenthal, Berkman, & Associates, 1967). The implication is that early and appropriate intervention to help families manage the stresses of caregiving more effectively can make home care a more viable alternative for a longer time. Our own experience shows that it is possible to keep a dementia patient at home, even when the disease is severe, and in some cases, until the patient's death. While stressful to family caregivers, the burden is not overwhelming, and they come away knowing they have done the best they could.

## SUMMARY

The goal of this book is to provide positive approaches for the assessment and treatment of senile dementia patients and their families. The prevailing myth is there is nothing that can be done, except to place the patient in a nursing home. Relocation, however, is not the only alternative. It can often be delayed or avoided. It is up to providers of community services to initiate a change in this long-held view and to help families find practical alternatives that serve the best interests of the patient and themselves.

# CHAPTER 2

# CAUSES OF MEMORY LOSS: ALZHEIMER'S DISEASE, OTHER DEMENTIAS, AND CONDITIONS WITH SIMILAR SYMPTOMS

Dementia refers to a syndrome of progressive impairment of memory and other cognitive abilities, which can have a variety of causes. Some of the causes are currently irreversible and some are potentially treatable. The most prevalent irreversible dementias are Alzheimer's disease and multi-infarct dementia.

Among the potentially reversible causes of dementia symptoms are drug reactions, infections, and metabolic disorders. There are also several conditions which resemble dementia, but their prognosis is typically better. These conditions include delirium, depression, the effects of head trauma, and changes due to the normal aging process. The critical task for practitioners is to be familiar with the types of problems that can be mistaken for irreversible dementia, and to learn how to identify potentially treatable conditions.

This chapter will describe the major types of dementia and conditions which resemble it. The next two chapters will differentiate the characteristics of irreversible dementia from other, treatable afflictions.

One obstacle to better diagnosis is that the terminology used to describe dementia and delirium is often confusing. Terms are poorly defined, or are used in different ways by different authors. Categories which had been used widely in the past such as chronic and acute organic brain syndrome are now considered imprecise and inexact (see Cummings & Benson, 1983). Other terms, such as confusion, have always been somewhat vague and misleading. As knowledge of dementia and related problems has increased, a more consistent, precise terminology has been emerging. The terms used here reflect current knowledge and are summarized in Table 2.1, along with those terms they have replaced.

An important consideration in defining dementia, delirium, and depression is to note that they are *syndromes*, rather than diseases. A syndrome is a cluster of symptoms which can have a variety of causes. As will be discussed later in this chapter, dementia and delirium can sometimes have the same causes. In some instances the cause cannot be definitively determined. Alzheimer's disease, for example, can only be confirmed as the cause of the dementia symptoms upon autopsy. In general, correct identification of which syndrome is present clarifies the next steps for assessment and treatment. It is also important not to confuse syndrome and disease, for instance, to assume that dementia and Alzheimer's disease are synonymous because that may lead to overlooking a potentially reversible cause.

## TYPES OF IRREVERSIBLE DEMENTIA

### Alzheimer's Disease

The most common type of illness involving dementia is senile dementia of the Alzheimer type (SDAT), or Alzheimer's disease, as it is commonly called. It has been estimated that between 50 and 60 percent of cases of dementia have brain pathologies characteristic of Alzheimer's disease (Terry & Wisniewski, 1977; Terry, 1978; Roth, 1980). Originally described in 1907 by Dr. Alois Alzheimer, this disorder was considered a dementia that affected people between the ages of 40 and 55. Studies done in the last 15 years have revealed that the type of brain pathology in cases of those younger than 65 is similar to that found in the majority of dementia patients with onset after 65. There continues to be speculation that early and late onset cases are different forms of

## CAUSES OF MEMORY LOSS

### TABLE 2.1
Definitions of Dementia, Delirium, Depression and Normal Aging

| Term | Definition | Other Names |
|---|---|---|
| Dementia | A syndrome involving memory and other impairments in cognition and behavior. Dementia may be irreversible when caused by a degenerative brain disease, or may be potentially reversible, if caused by treatable conditions such as metabolic or toxic disorders. | Dementing illness, organic brain syndrome (O.B.S.), chronic brain syndrome (C.B.S.), senility, senile dementia |
| Alzheimer's disease | The most frequent cause of irreversible dementia. | Senile dementia of the Alzheimer type (SDAT) Primary degenerative dementia |
| Multi-infarct dementia | A type of dementia caused by multiple small strokes (also called transient ischemic attacks or t.i.a.'s). | Vascular dementia |
| Delirium | A syndrome involving fluctuating mental function and disturbances of consciousness, attention, and cognition. Delirium can be caused by many conditions, including drugs, infections, fractures, metabolic disorders, malnutrition, and environmental stress. | Acute brain syndrome (A.B.S.), acute confusional state, toxic psychosis |
| Nonprogressive brain injury | Brain damage caused by head trauma, or other injury. Cognitive impairments depend on site and severity of the injury. Impairment does not get worse over time. | |
| Depression | Persistent feelings of sadness or dysphoric mood; often accompanied by lack of energy, loss of appetite, insomnia, withdrawal from usual activities. In the elderly, depression sometimes presents without overt complaints of sadness. | Depressive dementia, pseudodementia, dementia syndrome of depression, affective disorder, unipolar depression |
| Normal aging | The normal changes in behavior that occur with aging and in the absence of a dementing illness. These changes have a benign impact on cognitive functioning. | Senescence |

the disease. The clinical observation is often made that some cases having late onset have a more benign course (Cummings & Benson, 1983).

Alzheimer's disease is characterized by certain specific changes in the brain: senile plaques, neurofibrillary tangles, granulovacuolar structures, and an overall loss of neurons (Figure 2.1). These changes are not found or are found only to a limited degree in normal older persons (Roth, 1980).

The process of deterioration in a brain cell affected by Alzheimer's disease is illustrated in Figure 2.1. A normal brain cell (1) has a nucleus inside. The long projection radiating out from the cell that looks like the trunk of a tree is the axon. Electrochemical messages are transmitted from the cell body along the axon and then to other cells. The cells do not come into physical contact with one another; rather, the message is carried chemically across a gap called the synapse to the dendrites of another cell. The dendrites are the projections that look like roots and branches, and they receive messages from other neurons.

In Alzheimer's disease, abnormal tangled protein fibers, the neurofibrillary tangles, appear in the cell body (2). Usually, when there are tangles, there are also senile plaques nearby (2). Plaques are masses of degenerated cell matter which occur in the spaces between cells and interfere with the messages that are sent from cell to cell.

If you think of a normal cell (1) as a tree, then the tangles are like a disease from within and the plaques are like a pest outside. What happens to the cell is very much like what happens to a tree being defoliated (3), (4). It swells and becomes gnarled; then it shrivels (5) to a stump (6) (see Scheibel, 1983). The areas of the brain in which Alzheimer-type changes are found show a loss of neurons and other abnormalities.

The other characteristic change in Alzheimer's disease, the granulovacuolar structures, are sacs filled with fluid and granular material that accumulate in the cell bodies of pyramidal cells in the hippocampus but rarely in other parts of the brain. Thus, impairment resulting from Alzheimer's disease appears selective for certain areas of the brain and types of cells. According to

**FIGURE 2.1.**
Progressive Degeneration of a Brain Neuron in Alzheimer's Disease

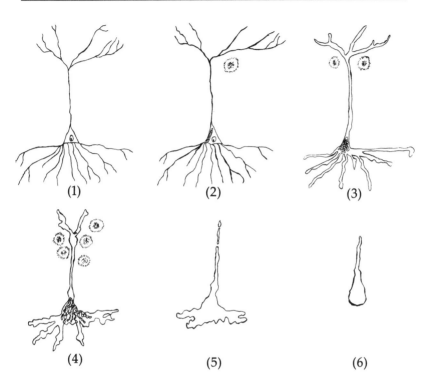

Cummings and Benson (1983), damaged neurons are found primarily in the posterotemporal, parietal, and frontal cortex, and in the hippocampus. Within these regions neurons in the cholinergic system appear especially affected.

The cause of the changes brought about by Alzheimer's disease is not known. There are currently several theories which are being investigated, but at present, none should be viewed as definitive. Among the possible causes that are being considered are genetic, viral, biochemical, immunological, and toxic. The possibility that Alzheimer's disease might be inherited has been raised by the observation of multiple cases in some families. Evidence of inheritance is primarily found when the age of onset of the dementia is before 55 (Mortimer, Schuman, & French,

1981). The genetic mechanisms are not known (Matsuyama, 1983), and the degree of risk to children of parents with Alzheimer's disease cannot be estimated at this time. The findings of changes in the brains of adults born with Down's syndrome and chromosomal abnormalities in Alzheimer patients also suggest possible genetic causes (Jarvik, 1978). The hypothesis that a slow-acting virus is the cause of the brain changes in SDAT is based in part on observations of viral transmission in two rare types of dementia, Jakob-Creutzfeldt disease and kuru, but transmission of Alzheimer's disease has not been demonstrated in laboratory studies. There is no reason to believe that the disease is contagious through ordinary contact with afflicted persons. Biochemical theories have been spurred by recent findings of deficits in the cholinergic system in the brains of patients afflicted with Alzheimer's disease, including selective losses of neurons and reduced production of the substance, choline acetyltransferase (Perry & Perry, 1983). (Attempts to increase it through ingestion of large amounts of its precursor, acetylcholine (lecithin), have not proven to be an effective treatment.) Another theory is that Alzheimer's disease is caused by immunological deficiencies (Nandy, 1983). Several abnormalities in the immune system of patients with Alzheimer's disease have been observed, but it is not known if these changes are a cause or consequence of the disease. Speculation about toxic causes was stimulated by reports of high levels of aluminum in the brains of Alzheimer victims, but further laboratory studies have failed to confirm these findings.

One other theory, proposed by the British geropsychiatrist Sir Martin Roth (1980), is that Alzheimer's disease is brought about by an accumulation of insults to the brain, rather than by any single cause. Clinical observations support this proposition, since the dementing process sometimes appears to begin following surgery in which a general anesthetic was used or after a head trauma was suffered. Contrary to early belief about dementia, Alzheimer's disease is not caused by hardening of the arteries or lack of oxygen to the brain, and increasing the

14

availability of oxygen has no effect on patients (Thompson, Davis, Obrist, & Heyman, 1976). For a more complete review of these theories, see Roth (1980) and Cummings and Benson (1983).

At present, clinical tests cannot definitively determine if symptoms of dementia are due to Alzheimer's disease (NIA Task Force, 1980). Only an autopsy or brain biopsy can confirm that symptoms are due to Alzheimer's disease. Because of this problem of diagnosis, the American Psychiatric Association in its Diagnostic and Statistical Manual recommends using the term "primary degenerative dementia," rather than Alzheimer's disease. Since it cannot be positively confirmed, practitioners should exercise some caution in labelling a case "Alzheimer's disease."

Alzheimer's disease has received a tremendous amount of attention in the media recently, and while this has helped generate public understanding and research, the negative effect has been that the label is being used indiscriminantly. In our experience, we have seen increasing numbers of people who were diagnosed as having Alzheimer's disease who had no dementia at all.

As has been mentioned, there is no effective medical cure for Alzheimer's disease. Among the treatments that have been tried are tranquilizing and stimulating medications, vasodilators, vitamins, hyperbaric oxygen, gerovital, and, as noted earlier, acetylcholine (Funkenstein, Hicks, Dysken, & Davis, 1981, Rosenberg, Greenwald, & Davis, 1983). Substances that are still being tried experimentally are nalaxone, choline (lecithin), and physostigmine. While it is advantageous to eat properly and exercise, there is no evidence nutritional programs or physical activity prevent or reverse the progress of dementia. Dementia patients should be maintained on an adequate diet, since poor nutrition can make symptoms worse.

The course of Alzheimer's disease generally involves a gradual deterioration in functioning. Various stages of the disease have been proposed by some authors. Reisberg and his associates (1982), for example, describe five stages involving progressive decline in cognitive and behavioral abilities. In the first stage, memory deficits are observed, along with mood disturbances (anxiety, depression). As memory worsens, there is a loss of ability to perform complex activities (stage 2). Stages 3 and 4 involve increased impairment of memory and the loss of ability to function independently. Eventually, all verbal and self-care abilities are lost (stage 5).

Although many cases follow this pattern, it may be premature to characterize well-defined stages of Alzheimer's disease, since many cases have somewhat different patterns of deterioration than described by Reisberg. There can be considerable variation in symptoms from one patient to another. More will be gained by careful observations of patients, than by characterizing them as falling into a particular stage.

The duration of the disease also varies from patient to patient. While early reports suggested that death occured four to five years after onset, patients with histories of the disease for ten years or more are not uncommon. Because a definitive diagnosis is usually not available, it is difficult to evaluate whether patients in which the disease develops either rapidly or slowly have different variants of Alzheimer's disease or different diseases altogether.

### Multi-infarct Dementia

The second most common cause of dementia is multi-infarct dementia, which postmortem studies have found to account for 10 to 20 percent of cases (Terry & Wisniewski, 1977; Terry, 1978). Multi-infarct dementia occurs when a person suffers a series of strokes or infarcts due to occlusions of arteries in the brain. Often the strokes are so small that there are no overt symptoms at the time they occur. On occasions, these patients also suffer a major stroke, involving paralysis and other impairments. People who have suffered strokes, however, do not invariably develop a dementia. The types of symptoms in multi-infarct dementia depend on the size of arteries which are blocked and the areas of the brain which are damaged (Cummings & Benson, 1983).

The causes of multi-infarct dementia are not known. It is believed that the same risk factors are involved as in heart disease and stroke, including high blood pressure, high cholesterol diet, overweight, smoking and lack of exercise. However, it is not clear why someone who is at risk develops a dementia and another person does not.

As with Alzheimer's disease, there are no known cures which reverse the damage caused by a multi-infarct dementia. However, treatment of other illnesses, such as high blood pressure, may mitigate further deterioration, especially in cases which are detected early (Roth, 1980).

Some persons with dementia have been found to have brain damage typical of both Alzheimer's disease and multi-infarct dementia. Autopsy studies have indicated that about 10 to 15 percent of all dementia cases are of a mixed type (Terry & Wisniewski, 1977).

### Rarer Types of Irreversible Dementia

In addition to Alzheimer's disease and multi-infarct dementia, there are a number of rarer diseases which can cause progressive memory impairment and other dementia symptoms. Pick's disease is perhaps the best known of these. While onset takes place typically between 40 and 60 years of age, cases of both younger and older people have been reported (Cummings & Benson, 1983). The course of the disease is estimated at six to 12 years. According to Cummings and Benson (1983), different areas of the brain are affected than in Alzheimer's disease. CT scans of patients suffering Alzheimer's disease show widespread atrophy in the cortex, while in patients suffering from Pick's disease the temporal and frontal lobes are primarily affected. There are also some differences in symptoms. Personality changes are more evident in early stages of Pick's disease, while memory loss and impairment in spatial abilities occur later. Patients with Pick's disease also manifest different language disturbances, including echolalia and the use of stereotyped language.

Other rare infectious diseases can lead to dementia, including Jakob-Creutzfeldt disease and kuru. General paresis can cause dementia, but the successful treatment of syphilis has made this condition increasingly rare.

The types of dementia discussed so far primarily affect the cortex, or in the case of multi-infarct dementia, can affect both cortical and subcortical regions of the brain. A number of diseases which principly affect subcortical areas can also lead to dementia. These include Parkinson's disease, Huntington's disease, progressive supranuclear palsy, Wilson's disease, spinocerebellar degenerations, and idiopathic basal ganglia calcification. For descriptions of these disorders, see Cummings and Benson (1983).

A major feature of the subcortical diseases is disturbances of motor functions, including posture, gait, and movement (Cummings & Benson, 1983). In Parkinson's disease, motor impairment is noticed first, and dementia may or may not develop as part of the subsequent course of the disease. Motor disturbances are rarer in Alzheimer's and Pick's disease, until late in the course of disease. A summary of types of irreversible dementia appear in Table 2.2.

Chronic alcoholism, also can result in dementia or memory impairment. In contrast to dementia, however, damage from alcohol is not progressive, if the person stops drinking.

## CONDITIONS MISTAKEN FOR IRREVERSIBLE DEMENTIA

Because many people believe that senility is an integral part of aging, any mental changes in an older person tend to be viewed as a symptom of dementia. But, in fact, there are several causes of mental changes which are frequently mistaken for irreversible dementia and which often respond to treatment. These reversible problems can be classified by their presenting symptoms as delirium, reversible dementia, depression, and nonprogressive brain damage. In addition, some mild change in memory which comes with normal aging can be mistaken for senility.

**TABLE 2.2.**
Types of Irreversible Dementia

**Disorders primarily affecting cortical regions of the brain**
Alzheimer's Disease
Pick's Disease

**Disorders with cortical and subcortical features**
Multi-infarct dementia
Infectious dementias—
  Jakob-Creutzfeldt disease
  Kuru
  General paresis

**Disorders primarily affecting subcortical regions of the brain**
Parkinson's disease
Huntington's disease
Progressive supranuclear palsy
Wilson's disease
Spinocerebellar degenerations
Idiopathic basal ganglia calcification

Adapted from J. L. Cummings & D. F. Benson, *Dementia: A Clinical Approach* (Boston: Butterworths, 1983), p. 8. By permission of the publisher.

## Delirium and Reversible Dementia

The terms "delirium" and "reversible dementia" refer to syndromes involving cognitive impairment that resemble senile dementia, but these are often brought about by conditions that can be treated. Delirium is marked by disturbed mental functioning which frequently includes dramatic symptoms such as hallucinations, delusions, disorientation, increased or decreased alertness, attention deficits, and disturbed sleep patterns. There are rapid fluctuations in symptoms and their severity. In contrast, reversible dementia has been described as involving symptoms of memory loss which are virtually indistinguishable from irreversible dementia (NIA Task Force, 1980), or in which features typical of subcortical dementia are present (Cummings & Benson, 1983). With proper treatment of the causes of a delirium or reversible dementia, recovery is often possible.

A recent task force of the National Institute of Aging has summarized the most frequent causes of delirium and reversible dementia in older persons (NIA Task Force, 1980). These include toxic effects of medications or interactions between drugs, brain tumor, infections, electrolyte imbalances, malnutrition, and metabolic and endocrine disorders (see Table 2.3). Symptoms may also occur following surgeries, fractures, head injuries, strokes, or environmental changes, including being moved to a nursing home or after the death of a spouse. As can be seen in Table 2.3, the same causes can sometimes lead to either symptoms of delirium or dementia. When the cause of the symptoms can be treated, the outcome is generally good, and complete recovery is not uncommon. If left untreated however, many of these conditions will lead to permanent brain damage and/or to death.

A condition causing potentially reversible dementia symptoms which has received considerable attention is hydrocephalus. This disorder involves obstruction in the flow of cerebrospinal fluid. Hydrocephalus is identified when the patient displays three symptoms: disturbed gait, a slowing of mental functioning including mild to severe memory loss, and incontinence (Cummings & Benson, 1983). Further evidence of hydrocephalus comes from CT scans. Enlargement of the ventricles, especially in the frontal and temporal areas can suggest hydrocephalus. Treatment involves a surgical procedure of placing a shunt in the brain to drain the excess fluid. Successful treatment can result in considerable reversal of symptoms, but there are a variety of potential complications. Overall, the success rate has been estimated as between 45 and 55 percent (Katzman, 1977; Cummings & Benson, 1983). Although the causes of hydrocephalus in adulthood and old age are sometimes unknown, head trauma, tumors and brain inflammations or infections can be contributing factors.

The following is a case example in which a delirium was mistaken for irreversible dementia.

A retired 75-year-old school teacher with no previous history of mental problems began complaining to her son that people were tapping her telephone, and were plotting to overthrow the government. She believed

# CAUSES OF MEMORY LOSS

**TABLE 2.3.**
Reversible Causes of Dementia Symptoms and Delirium

| | Dementia | Delirium | Either or Both |
|---|---|---|---|
| Therapeutic drug intoxication | | | Yes |
| Depression | Yes | | |
| Metabolic | | | |
|   a. Azolemia or renal failure (dehydration, diuretics, obstruction, hypokalemia) | | | Yes |
|   b. Hyponatremia (diuretics, excess antidiuretic hormone, salt wasting, intravenous fluids) | | | Yes |
|   c. Hypernatremia (dehydration, intravenous saline) | | Yes | |
|   d. Volume depletion (diuretics, bleeding, inadequate fluids) | | | Yes |
|   e. Acid-base disturbance | | Yes | |
|   f. Hypoglycemia (insulin, oral hypoglycemics, starvation) | | | Yes |
|   g. Hyperglycemia (diabetic ketoacidosis, or hyperosmolar coma) | | Yes | |
|   h. Hepatic failure | | | Yes |
|   i. Hypothyroidism | | | Yes |
|   j. Hyperthyroidism (especially apathetic) | | | Yes |
|   k. Hypercalcemia | | | Yes |
|   l. Cushing's syndrome | Yes | | |
|   m. Hypopituitarism | | | Yes |
| Infection, fever, or both | | | |
|   a. Viral | | | Yes |
|   b. Bacterial | | | |
|     Pneumonia | | Yes | |
|     Pyelonephritis | | Yes | |
|     Cholecystitis | | Yes | |
|     Diverticulitis | | Yes | |
|     Tuberculosis | | | Yes |
|     Endocarditis | | | Yes |
| Cardiovascular | | | |
|   a. Acute myocardial infarct | | Yes | |
|   b. Congestive heart failure | | | Yes |
|   c. Arrhythmia | | | Yes |
|   d. Vascular occlusion | | | Yes |
|   e. Pulmonary embolus | | Yes | |

TABLE 2.3. (Continued)

| | Dementia | Delirium | Either or Both |
|---|---|---|---|
| Brain disorders | | | |
| a. Vascular insufficiency | | | |
| Transient ischemia | | Yes | |
| Stroke | | | Yes |
| b. Trauma | | | |
| Subdural hematoma | | | Yes |
| Concussion/confusion | | Yes | |
| Intracerebral hemorrhage | | Yes | |
| Epidural hematoma | | Yes | |
| c. Infection | | | |
| Acute meningitis (pyogenic, viral) | | Yes | |
| Chronic meningitis (tuberculous, fungal) | | | Yes |
| Neurosyphilis | | | Yes |
| Subdural empyema | | | Yes |
| Brain abscess | | | Yes |
| d. Tumors | | | |
| Metastatic to brain | | | Yes |
| Primary in brain | | | Yes |
| e. Normal pressure hydrocephalus | Yes | | |
| Pain | | | |
| a. Fecal impaction | | | Yes |
| b. Urinary retention | | Yes | |
| c. Fracture | | Yes | |
| d. Surgical abdomen | | Yes | |
| Sensory deprivation states such as blindness or deafness | | | Yes |
| Hospitalization | | | |
| a. Anesthesia or surgery | | | Yes |
| b. Environmental change and isolation | | | Yes |
| Alcohol toxic reactions | | | |
| a. Lifelong alcoholism | Yes | | |
| b. Alcoholism new in old age | | | Yes |
| c. Decreased tolerance with age producing increasing intoxication | | | Yes |
| d. Acute hallucinosis | | Yes | |
| e. Delirium tremens | | Yes | |
| Anemia | | | Yes |
| Tumor—systemic effects of nonmetastatic malignant neoplasm | | | Yes |
| Chronic lung disease with hypoxia or hypercapnia | | | Yes |

TABLE 2.3. (Continued)

| | Dementia | Delirium | Either or Both |
|---|---|---|---|
| Deficiencies of nutrients such as vitamin B$_{12}$, folic acid, or niacin | Yes | | |
| Accidental hypothermia | | Yes | |
| Chemical intoxications | | | |
| a. Heavy metals such as arsenic, lead, or mercury | | | Yes |
| b. Consciousness-altering agents | | | Yes |
| c. Carbon monoxide | | | Yes |

From NIA Task Force, "Senility Reconsidered," *Journal of the American Medical Association* (October, 1980).

that she was the only person who could save the country. Her son regarded these delusions as evidence of senility and took steps to have her placed in a nursing home. In the meantime, however, he placed her in the geropsychiatric unit of an acute care hospital. A medical workup was done, which revealed a kidney infection. Treatment of the kidney problem resulted in cessation of the delusions and complete recovery.

It is important to consider that someone with an irreversible dementia can also develop a delirium. In fact, they may be more susceptible to a delirium than someone with normal brain functioning. This means that someone with a progressive brain disease is more vulnerable to the effects of drugs and the various illnesses shown in Table 2.3 which cause a delirium (Lipowski, 1980). This problem is compounded by the fact that dementia patients seldom report physical symptoms, and so an illness might go unnoticed. Any sudden or dramatic change in behavior of the patient raises the issue of an underlying, treatable problem.

The following is an example of someone with an irreversible dementia who developed a drug-induced delirium.

The husband of a 77-year-old woman with a ten-year history of progressive impairment complained that his wife's symptoms had recently changed for the worse. She was now having angry outbursts and hallucinatory experiences, especially in the evening. She had been taking a stimulant, Ritalin (methlyphenidate), for some time, which had been prescribed to treat her cognitive impairment (though with little effect). When these new symptoms were first manifested, the prescribing physician recommended doubling the dose. Symptoms increased markedly after that. Because she was on a medication that can become toxic, and since symptoms worsened after the drug was increased, the drug was considered a likely cause. Taking her off the medication resulted in total cessation of the hallucinations and outbursts within one week. A six month followup indicated no recurrence of these symptoms.

In our experience, the drugs most commonly prescribed for dementia patients, major and minor tranquilizers, sometimes have similar effects. These medications are typically prescribed for restlessness, agitation or sleeplessness, and while some initial benefits may occur, the drugs may quickly build up to toxic levels, making symptoms that the drug is meant to treat worse. A theme we will return to throughout this book is that maintaining dementia patients on small amounts of drugs or even none at all is an important part of any care.

## Nonprogressive Brain Damage

There are many causes of brain damage which are not progressive. These include injuries from head trauma, strokes, and aneurysms. The impairment caused by these problems tends to be selective, rather than global. This means some abilities are affected, but others are unchanged. These impairments also usually remain stable.

Because the symptoms that are apparent in cases of brain damage are often similar to those shown by dementia, including impairment of memory, attention, and judgment, the possibility of nonprogressive brain damage as a cause is often overlooked. It is important to differentiate nonprogressive from progressive conditions because they have dramatically different implications for both the patient and family. For instance, the patient can often compensate for cognitive problems caused by the brain damage by using abilities which have not been affected. It is also important for the patient and family to know that the brain damage is not going to progress.

As noted earlier, head trauma or stroke can sometimes set off a degenerative dementia. In our experience this is relatively rare, but the possibility should not be overlooked. The doctor or service provider therefore should know that this type of brain damage is usually stable, but if symptoms appear to be worsening, the causes of that change should be investigated.

## Depression

Depression is often difficult to distinguish from irreversible dementia in the elderly. Many symptoms are present in both. Depressed persons resemble dementia patients because they are often mentally and physically slow in their responses, show little or no interest in their surroundings, and have withdrawn from their usual activities. Furthermore, many depressed people also complain of memory loss. In contrast to dementia, however, memory changes brought about by depression are mild. Depressed people appear to focus on normal incidents which anyone might forget and magnify their importance. A dementia patient, however, will often deny memory problems, or will say, "I have a memory problem," but will not be able to give specific examples (Kahn, Zarit, Hilbert, & Niederehe, 1975; Orr, Reever, & Zarit, 1980; S. Zarit, 1982).

The importance of distinguishing between dementia and depression is that depressed older persons improve with treatment. Antidepressant medications are sometimes effective. Structured psychotherapies developed for treatment of depression such as Beck's cognitive therapy (Beck, Rush, Shaw, & Emery, 1979) or Lewinsohn's behavioral treatment (Lewinsohn, Munoz, Youngren, & Zeiss, 1978) have been found to be effective with older, depressed patients, both in conjunction with medications, or alone (Gallagher & Thompson, 1983).

Another consideration is that dementia and depression do not always occur separately. Depression is often present in early stages of the dementing illness. In these cases the cognitive impairment will presumably get worse, whereas when dementia is not present, cognitive complaints associated with depression will lessen as mood improves (Popkin, Thompson, Gallagher, &

Moore, 1982). Whenever mild memory loss and depression are found, treatment for the latter should be considered. Even if it ultimately turns out that the cognitive symptoms are due to dementia, treating the depression may improve some aspects of the person's functioning.

## Normal Aging

Because many people believe that everyone who is old is senile, the mental changes that occur with aging are often mistaken for dementia. The normal aging process, however, does not affect an individual's competency or ability to care for himself. In fact, changes in memory and other intellectual abilities are relatively mild when there is no dementing illness. Often accumulated information and experience compensate for changes in memory function.

The principle change occurring in memory with normal aging is a slowing in the time necessary for learning and recalling information. An older person may also be distracted more easily, which affects the capacity for learning and memory. These changes, however, do not indicate an inability to learn or remember. Rather, they suggest older people need to take more time and effort to remember. There is, of course, no reason to believe that the healthy older person (with a normal memory) will be unable to manage his or her affairs.

Some older people react to incidents of forgetfulness by believing they are becoming senile. Sometimes people who observe an older person forget something assume that it is due to senility as well. But occasional forgetfulness is common at any age. Problems remembering a name, or where you put something in the house, or an item you wanted to buy at the store are reported by young persons as well as the more elderly. These are the most common complaints of older persons. The fact is that occasional forgetting is normal, irrespective of age (S. Zarit, 1982).

The changes associated with normal aging are mild. There is no reason to treat most aged persons as if they are in the process of becoming mentally incompetent. The distinction between normal aging and dementia is one of the most important for medical staff, and anyone else for that matter, to make.

## SUMMARY

The term *dementia* refers to any of several progressive and degenerative brain disorders. These diseases result in severe memory loss and other intellectual impairments. In a given case, it is not always possible to identify the type of dementia with current diagnostic procedures. A more important consideration in the diagnosis of dementia is to rule out the many treatable conditions that can cause symptoms that resemble dementia.

# CHAPTER 3

# HOW TO ASSESS FOR DEMENTIA

Assessing patients involves two processes. First, the clinician must determine what type of problem is present. This chapter will present practical steps for assessing persons with complaints of cognitive impairments and for differentiating dementia from the disorders which resemble it. The second process involves gathering the additional information necessary for making psychosocial interventions, which will be addressed in the next chapter.

A critical factor in assessing a person with dementia-like symptoms is to determine if there may be some problem causing the symptoms that can be treated. The syndromes which need to be differentiated from irreversible dementia are shown in Figure 3.1. A careful medical and psychosocial evaluation of patients combined with reports from family or other informants will reveal these possible causes of symptoms.

Assessment of dementia can be a difficult process because of all the factors one must consider in evaluating a patient with memory loss. There are no tests which can definitively diagnose Alzheimer's disease or other common types of dementia or rule them out. Instead the practitioner must weigh evidence from several sources.

From time to time everyone will make errors in assessment, and so it is important to consider the implications of these errors. Kahn and Miller (1978) have described two possible errors in evaluating older patients. The first type of error is failing to diagnose an irreversible dementia when it is present. They suggest this type of error has minimal consequences. Because there are

**FIGURE 3.1.**
Differentiating Dementia from Treatable Conditions

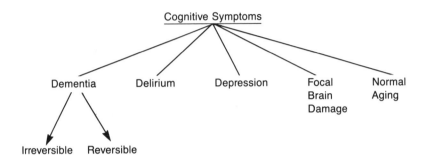

currently no cures, the patient is not denied appropriate care. The second type of error is to diagnose an irreversible dementia when it is not present. This type of error can have serious consequences. It can generate a sense of hopelessness about the patient, such that treatable causes will not be evaluated. Under these circumstances, family, friends, medical personnel, and even patients themselves, will give up on any possibility of change. For that reason, Kahn and Miller argue that diagnosis of dementia must be conservative. Dementia should be diagnosed only when there is unequivocable evidence and when other, treatable causes have been ruled out.

General criteria for diagnosis of dementia, delirium, and depression are presented in the Third Edition of *The Diagnostic and Statistical Manual* of the American Psychiatric Association, or the *DSM* III, 1980 (see Table 3.1). These definitions briefly describe each syndrome. The definition of dementia is based on a loss of intellectual abilities which interferes with social activities or work, memory impairment, other cognitive deficits such as impairment of abstract thinking and judgment, personality change, confirming history, and the absence of evidence of delirium, intoxication, or other possible medical and psychiatric causes of the symptoms.

Delirium is characterized by "clouding of consciousness," which is described as "reduced clarity of awareness of the envi-

# HOW TO ASSESS FOR DEMENTIA

**TABLE 3.1.**
DSM III Criteria for Dementia and Delirium

**Diagnostic criteria for Dementia**
A. A loss of intellectual abilities of sufficient severity to interfere with social or occupational functioning.

B. Memory impairment.

C. At least one of the following:

> (1) impairment of abstract thinking, as manifested by concrete interpretation of proverbs, inability to find similarities and differences between related words, difficulty in defining words and concepts, and other similar tasks

> (2) impaired judgment

> (3) other disturbances of higher cortical function, such as aphasia (disorder of language due to brain dysfunction), apraxia (inability to carry out motor activities despite intact comprehension and motor function), agnosia (failure to recognize or identify objects despite intact sensory function), "constructional difficulty" (e.g., inability to copy three-dimensional figures, assemble blocks, or arrange sticks in specific designs)

> (4) personality change, i.e., alteration or accentuation of premorbid traits

D. State of consciousness not clouded (i.e., does not meet the criteria for Delirium or Intoxication, although these may be superimposed).

E. Either (1) or (2):
> (1) evidence from the history, physical examination, or laboratory tests, of a specific organic factor that is judged to be etiologically related to the disturbance

> (2) in the absence of such evidence, an organic factor necessary for the development of the syndrome can be presumed if conditions other than Organic Mental Disorders have been reasonably excluded and if the behavioral change represents cognitive impairment in a variety of areas

**Diagnostic criteria for Delirium**
A. Clouding of consciousness (reduced clarity of awareness of the environment), with reduced capacity to shift, focus, and sustain attention to environmental stimuli.

B. At least two of the following:

> (1) perceptual disturbance: misinterpretations, illusions, or hallucinations

31

TABLE 3.1. (Continued)

---

(2) speech that is at times incoherent

(3) disturbance of sleep-wakefulness cycle, with insomnia or daytime drowsiness

(4) increased or decreased psychomotor activity

C. Disorientation and memory impairment (if testable).

D. Clinical features that develop over a short period of time (usually hours to days) and tend to fluctuate over the course of a day.

E. Evidence, from the history, physical examination, or laboratory tests, or a specific organic factor judged to be etiologically related to the disturbance.

From *Diagnostic and statistical manual of mental disorders. 3rd Ed.* (Washington, D.C.: American Psychiatric Association, 1980), pp. 107, 111–112. Used with permission.

---

ronment" (*DSM* III, 1980). Other features are an attentional deficit, illusions, hallucinations, occasionally incoherent speech, extreme drowsiness or insomnia, increased or decreased motor activity, disorientation and memory impairment, and a history of a short duration and fluctuation of symptoms.

While providing general guidelines, the criteria for dementia and delirium do not specify the operational steps involved in making a decision about diagnosis. For example, how much "memory impairment" must be present to suggest dementia? Since there is a certain amount of forgetting that occurs normally, and some increase in this "benign" forgetfulness with age, there needs to be some norms for what constitutes memory impairment typical of dementia.

This chapter will provide the practitioner with operational guidelines for identifying possible cases of dementia. These guidelines represent a synthesis of the current understanding of dementia, and incorporate the caution against overdiagnosis suggested by Kahn and Miller. Three types of assessments will be stressed: 1. determination of current symptoms; 2. history of current problems; and 3. mental status testing. How to conduct and evaluate a psychosocial assessment and coordinate the findings with a medical examination are discussed below.

## PSYCHOSOCIAL ASSESSMENT OF SENILE DEMENTIA

### Determination of Current Symptoms

**Memory.** A clinical assessment should be done for any person suspected of having memory problems. A good place to begin is to ask that person about memory loss. For example, "Have you been having any problems with your memory?" People who complain about memory loss *often do not have* a dementia. This is particularly the case when they can give specific information of what and when they forget. Although complaining of memory loss, they are usually experiencing normal, everyday instances of forgetting. Depressed people, in particular, are likely to exaggerate these normal instances of forgetting. They will complain of difficulty concentrating, being absentminded, or making everyday mistakes, such as misplacing keys. When the practitioner inquires, the patient can usually provide a lot of specific information, including when the forgetting started, how often things are forgotten, and what things are forgotten. It usually turns out the frequency with which these problems occur is low, and no major incidents such as getting lost or forgetting how to perform well-learned activities are reported. (A person who has suffered a head trauma, stroke, or other nonprogressive brain damage may also complain of memory loss.)

In contrast, someone with dementia will often deny having memory problems, or if they admit it they can give very little information about when, what, and how often they forget. Often their affect is inappropriate in responding to questions about memory loss. They either have a blasé, unconcerned attitude, or in rarer instances, respond with anger or crying. They may find excuses for the problems they are having. (For example, they may say they cannot remember the date today because they did not look at a paper) or will blame others for causing them to forget. The reason dementia patients deny memory problems or are unable to recall specific instances is that as the disease progresses, their memory impairment becomes so severe that they can no longer remember that they have forgotten anything. An exception is that someone with early, mild symptoms of dementia may be aware of memory loss. Patients with a delirium may also deny having memory problems, or will have periods of clear mental functioning in which they are aware of their memory problems.

The implication is that the practioner should not take self-reports of memory loss at face value. The presence or absence of memory complaints is useful for generating hypotheses about what type of problem is present. More information, especially history and memory testing, is needed to clarify the meaning of the complaints.

**Hallucinations and Delusions.** Among the symptoms most upsetting to the patient's family or friends are hallucinations or delusions. Hallucinations involve seeing or hearing things that are not present. One patient, for instance, claimed to see little children running by, and would call them, or try to reach out to them. Delusions are distortions of reality. The old, retired school teacher cited in the last chapter who believed there was a plot to overthrow the government is an example of someone with delusional beliefs.

Hallucinations and delusions are sometimes mistakenly considered typical of dementia, but are more common in cases of delirium (Lipowski, 1980; Cummings & Benson, 1983; Zarit, 1980). Some dementia patients with mild degrees of cognitive impairment will make accusations about their possessions having been stolen. These accusations appear to be an attempt to cover up the inability to remember where the misplaced items are. The symptoms usually do not reach the magnitude where the patient reports a complicated plot or other elaborate paranoid belief system. More severely impaired individuals will report "illusions," a very mild form of hallucination; for example, they report seeing a small animal or something else moving across the room. These impressions are fleeting and are often in response to changing conditions of illumination. The person seems unable to interpret the changes in light and shadow correctly, and "fills in" an incorrect image. Illusions are more common in the evening.

When more dramatic or persistent evidence of delusions or hallucinations is present, a delirium or delirium combined with a dementia is suggested. Many of the common causes of delirium, such as drug toxicities, kidney or bladder infections, or malnutrition, can produce periods of hallucinations or delusions. Similarly, the appearance of hallucinations or delusions in someone with a history of dementia suggests a possible delirium that might be treatable. People sometimes overlook these problems and assume it is just part of the dementia. In our experience, reactions to medications including those drugs which have antipsychotic or tranquilizing properties are the most common cause of delirium in dementia patients. Medications such as Haldol (haloperidol) or Mellaril (thioridazine) can quickly build up to toxic levels, causing hallucinations and delusions, among other problems.

When a patient has hallucinations or delusions, two other possibilities besides those discussed above should be considered. The first is to determine if the person has had a lifelong history of schizophrenia, including recurrent episodes of similar symptoms and hospitalizations. The second is to find out if the person has held persistent paranoid beliefs for the first time in later life that are not due to delirium or dementia. (This is called "late life paranoid state," or "paraphrenia.") The possible etiologies of this syndrome include bilateral hearing loss and an exacerbation of a long-standing personality disorder (Zarit, 1980). Increased social isolation may be involved in the etiology of some paranoid disorders.

**Restlessness and Agitation.** Other problems considered typical of dementia are restlessness and agitation. While these symptoms sometimes occur in the course of the dementing illness, they also can be side effects of medications, or the result of low levels of activity. Tranquilizing medications are given to treat restlessness and agitation and may have initial positive effects.

When the level of dosage is not carefully monitored, however, the opposite effects can result, and the patient can become increasingly restless or agitated. Dementia patients maintained without drugs or on low dosages do not have these problems as often. In contrast to dementia patients, someone with a delirium may be extremely active, or extremely withdrawn, or may alternate between both even during the same day.

**Mood.** Mood changes may occur with all syndromes we have been describing. Dysphoric mood is, of course, the central, defining characteristic of depression. Dementia patients usually have flat or labile moods, but they sometimes can be depressed or anxious as well. Depression is often observed early in a dementia when cognitive deficits are still mild and the patient may have some awareness of current problems. Persons who have suffered head injuries may also be depressed or will have catastrophic reactions when they encounter frustrating situations. With delirium, mood fluctuates widely, from depression, anxiety, and euphoria, to an indifferent nonchalant mood.

**Personality Changes.** Personality changes also often accompany dementia. According to Butler and Lewis (1982), these changes may include reactions to memory loss and what they term "release phenomena," that is, a reduction in inhibitions restricting antisocial behavior. Reactions to memory loss can include denial, covering up, blaming others for taking or misplacing items, or getting extremely upset. Some examples of release phenomena include letting out anger, crying, inappropriate table manners, and inappropriate displays of sexuality. It should be noted that some dementia patients maintain adequate social skills, and can present a facade of normalcy even after the disease has become severe. In some cases, personality changes may precede memory impairment.

Changes similar to those that appear in dementia are sometimes present in delirium, especially denial and release behavior. Personality remains intact in cases of depression and normal aging. With head trauma, personality changes may be present, depending on the site and severity of the damage.

There are many other symptoms of dementia. We have highlighted only some examples, but others which might be present are impaired judgment and reasoning, speech disturbances, gait problems, and other motor changes. One of the characteristics of dementia is that it is extremely variable and that these symptoms can occur in any combination. A summary of the symptoms of dementia, delirium, focal brain damage, depression, and normal aging, appears in Table 3.2.

## History

A clinical history of the development of symptoms is perhaps the most reliable way to distinguish dementia from delirium, depression, head traumas, and normal aging. Dementia typically has an insidious onset, with gradual progression of symptoms. Delirium, in contrast, usually has a sudden onset. Depression tends either to be episodic or chronic, but in contrast to dementia, there is no report of gradual worsening of symptoms over time. There are memory changes and other alterations with normal aging, but these are not severe, and progression is barely noticeable from year to year. In cases of head trauma, onset of symptoms is associated with a specific injury.

A reliable informant is usually needed to obtain a good history. Although someone with depression can give an accurate report of his history, patients with delirium or dementia cannot. Clearly, obtaining a good history is more difficult when the impaired person lives alone and has only sporadic contact with other people. A good history involves determining when problems first started; the nature of the problems; subsequent changes; and finally the personal, medical, or environmental events associated with onset and progression of symptoms. Some suggested questions to include in the history are shown in Table 3.3.

A spouse, child, other relative or friend can provide the history. Some informants who have frequent contact with the patient, however, are poor historians. Nevertheless, practitioners should still try to get the information—it might still be of some value. With a poor historian the interviewer should patiently

**TABLE 3.2.**
A Summary of Assessment Procedures

| | Dementia | Delirium | Reversible Dementia | Focal Brain Damage | Depression | Normal Aging |
|---|---|---|---|---|---|---|
| **1. Current Symptoms** | | | | | | |
| a. Complaints of Memory Problems | Reported by others; patient often unaware | Patient often denies problems | Reported by others; patient often unaware | Patient may complain of memory loss | Patient usually complains of memory problems | Patient may complain of memory loss |
| b. Types of Memory Problems Reported | Major—interfere with activities of daily living | May be selective and variable; major activities disrupted | Major—interfere with activities of daily living | Specific functions more affected (e.g. spatial abilities but not verbal abilities or vice versa) | Mild, mostly due to inattention | Mild increase in normal forgetting (e.g. names) |
| c. Hallucinations and Delusions | Paranoid accusations sometimes present with mild memory loss; Illusions in severe cases | Sometimes vivid hallucinations and well-developed delusions are present | Not described well in the literature | Absent | Absent, except in extremely severe cases | Absent |
| **2. History** | | | | | | |
| a. Onset | SDAT: insidious Multi-infarct: sometimes sudden | Usually sudden | Not described well in the literature | Sudden, associated with brain trauma | Coincides with life changes; onset often abrupt | Reactions to normal life changes; no specific aging pattern |

| | | | | | | |
|---|---|---|---|---|---|---|
| b. Duration | Months or years | A few days or weeks | Not described well in the literature | Dates from incident | At least two weeks; can be several months or years | Minimal change over long periods of time |
| c. Progression | SDAT: Gradual Multi-infarct: Step-wise | Prodromal symptoms become severe in a few days | Not described well in the literature | Not progressive | Not progressive | Not progressive |
| d. Fluctuations | SDAT: Little Multi-infarct: Some daily fluctuation, usually worse in evening | Can be extreme, even from hour to hour | Not described well in the literature | Little | Typically worse in the morning | Mild situational fluctuations |
| 3. Tests<br>a. MSQ | Two or more errors | Connotative errors may be present | Two or more errors | Usually none or one error, unless damage is severe | Usually none or one error | Usually none or one error |
| b. Face-hand | Errors after fourth trial | May make errors after fourth trial | Errors after fourth trial | No, or unilateral errors | No errors after fourth trial | No errors after fourth trial |
| c. Neuropsychological | Severe global deficit | Selective impairment, especially attention | Not described well in the literature | Only certain abilities affected, depending on site of damage | Normal aging pattern; speeded tests may be lower | Normal aging pattern |

**TABLE 3.2.** (Continued)

| | Dementia | Delirium | Reversible Dementia | Focal Brain Damage | Depression | Normal Aging |
|---|---|---|---|---|---|---|
| d. Memory & Behavior Problems Checklist | Mild to extensive impairment | Mild to extensive impairment | Not described well in the literature | Usually only a few problems present | No, or a few problems | No, or a few problems |
| e. Caregiver's Burden | Mild to severe | Not determined | Mild to severe | Absent or mild | Mild to severe | If present, related to long-standing relationship problems or physical disability |

From S. H. Zarit & J. M. Zarit, "Cognitive impairment." In P. M. Lewinsohn & L. Teri (Eds.), *Clinical Geropsychology* (New York: Pergamon, 1983).

**TABLE 3.3.**
History of the Dementia
___

1. When did you first notice changes in the patient? (How long ago?)
2. What was the first sign?
3. What happened next and when?
4. Would you describe the onset as gradual or sudden?
5. When was it first diagnosed by a doctor?
6. What was the diagnosis?
7. Do you remember what tests were done? (Ask specifically about CAT Scan and its findings).
8. What drugs have been prescribed for this condition?
9. What are the current medications the patient is taking?
10. Has the course of the disease been gradual or stepwise?
11. Has the patient had any surgeries in recent years?
12. Has the patient had any head injuries in recent years?
13. Has anyone else in your family had a problem like this?

persist and reframe questions in several ways in order to pinpoint specific details as much as possible.

**History in Dementia Patients.** A typical history in dementia is a gradual onset of symptoms. Informants report that what they noticed first was an increase in the normal sorts of forgetting. These include misplacing items in the house, forgetting appointments, or misplacing keys. At first the informant regarded these changes as normal because everyone experiences some forgetting. But gradually the amount of forgetting increased and new problems appeared, such as the inability to handle money or balance a checkbook; inability to complete complex activities or follow through with directions and getting lost. The patient may begin asking the same question over and over again, unaware that he asked it before. Personality changes are also frequently reported and sometimes are the first symptoms that are noticed.

Some cases of dementia may have a more rapid onset than others. Specifically, a multi-infarct dementia may develop at the time the person suffers a series of small strokes. The course for multi-infarct dementia is also somewhat different. While symptoms typically progress, they do so in a stepwise fashion. That means that a patient will function at a stable level for an undetermined amount of time, and then will experience further decline. After each decline, the person usually stabilizes at that level.

There tend to be some day-to-day fluctuations in symptoms in all dementia patients. Symptoms tend to be worse at night, but changes can also be related to environmental or emotional factors. For example, some patients improve when company visits, and others become worse. Fluctuations tend to be greater in cases of multi-infarct dementia. Some persons have been observed to approach normal levels of cognitive functioning during good periods, even though they have had the disease for several years.

**History in Delirium and Reversible Dementia.** In contrast to dementias, most deliriums come on suddenly. The patient usually has had a history of adequate adjustment, but experiences dramatic changes over a period of a few days to a few weeks. In other words, changes are of recent onset. There can also be marked fluctuations of symptoms over the course of a day. At times the patient may be alert and rational; at other times, he may be drowsy, disoriented, or have hallucinatory experiences. A history of recent changes in lifestyle or habits will often indicate a possible reason for the delirium. For instance, the observation that a patient was recently started on a new medication suggests a drug reaction as a potential cause.

Some cases of delirium have been reported to come on very gradually, such as those caused by pernicious anemia. Reversible dementias may come on either gradually or suddenly. The implication is that whenever a patient has experienced sudden and recent changes, whether typical of delirium or dementia, all the more effort must be made to find a reversible cause. But even when the onset is gradual, the possibility of a reversible cause should be investigated.

As noted previously, someone with an irreversible dementia can develop a delirium. This is often indicated by a sudden worsening of cognitive or behavioral problems. The same symptoms which characterize a delirium in persons without dementia will be found in someone with delirium *and* dementia. Sometimes physicians and other professionals mistakenly assume that this is the next stage of the dementia. When there is a sudden change, however, the patient should be evaluated for a treatable cause of the new problems.

Dementia patients will sometimes develop a delirium in response to major changes in the environment. Recent moves, death of a spouse, and other major life events have been observed to cause delirium symptoms in someone with dementia. Given time and reassurance, these patients will show improvement, sometimes returning to their previous level of functioning. Surgery in which a general anesthetic was used is also frequently followed by a delirium, but there is less recovery of cognitive function than if other forms of stress are encountered. Clinical observations suggest some dementia patients have markedly worse behavioral and cognitive deficits following surgery.

**History in Depression.** Depressions in later life often follow either of two patterns: episodic or chronic. The onset of an episodic depression can be traced to a specific point in time. Symptoms of episodic depression often appear after major life changes, such as deaths of close relatives and friends, loss of job or income, or family conflict. With chronic depression, the other pattern, changes may date back several years, but in contrast to those of dementia, the symptoms do not become progressively worse.

**History in Head Trauma.** Head trauma can also be differentiated from dementia on the basis of history. Symptoms have their onset at the time of the injury, and typically do not become worse over time. Our experience is that head injuries often are overlooked as the cause of current problems.

**Normal Aging.** While cognitive changes occur in normal aging, these are barely perceptible from year to year. Healthy older persons typically report changes in memory compared to how they were 30 and 40 years ago. While these recollections may be somewhat idealized, neither the individual nor informants are likely to report significantly different changes in the past few years. A summary of the role of history in the assessment for dementia appears in Table 3.2.

## Testing

**Mental Status Testing.** A brief test of mental status can often help distinguish between dementia, delirium, and depression. Several mental status tests have been developed for use in evaluating cognitive deficits, including the Mental Status Questionnaire (Kahn, Goldfarb, Pollack, & Peck, 1960), the Short Portable Mental Status Questionnaire (Pfeiffer, 1975), and the Mini Mental State (Folstein, Folstein, & McHugh, 1975). A typical mental status test, such as the one shown in Table 3.4, asks questions such as "Where are you?," "What is the date today?," and "Who is President of the United States?" The advantage of relying on these questions is persons who make errors have major

**TABLE 3.4.**
Mental Status Questionnaire

1. Where are you now? (If the initial response is not complete, clarify with What place is this? What is the name of this place? What kind of place is this?
2. Where is it located? (approximate address)
3. What is the date today? Day?
4. Month?
5. Year?
6. How old are you?
7. When were you born? Month?
8. Year?
9. Who is president of the United States?
10. Who was president before him?

Additional Questions

Have you ever been in this place before?
Who am I? What do I do? (What is my job called)?
Have you ever seen me before?
Where were you last night?

Adapted from R. L. Kahn, A. I. Goldfarb, M. Pollack, & A. Peck, Brief objective measures for the determination of mental status in the aged, *American Journal of Psychiatry*, 1960, *117*, 326–328. Copyright 1960 by the American Psychiatric Association. Reprinted by permission.

and obvious deficits. However, the tests are not sensitive to the mild deficits that are present in early stages of dementia. These procedures are simple to use, and they are not usually skewed by education or motivation. Therefore, there are few false positive results of diagnosing dementia when it is not, in fact, present.

Because no one test will always be accurate, test results are best relied upon as another source of evidence to be evaluated alongside history and current symptoms. Test scores should never be used themselves for making a diagnosis. While the number of correct or incorrect answers is important, qualitative differences in responses should also be considered, as will be discussed below.

When testing someone, it is important to put that person at ease and to explain what will be happening. We often introduce mental status testing by asking the patient about his memory, and then finding out if it would be acceptable to ask some questions involving memory. Dementia patients usually do not get upset during testing, but if that does happen, the interviewer can respond by providing reassurance and by slowing down.

Dementia is suggested when someone makes two or more errors on the numbered items in the Mental Status Questionnaire shown in Table 3.4. The patient may give incorrect information, or say he does not know. Some patients may give excuses for not knowing information. One woman, for instance, said she would look up the date when she got home. This kind of response is a way of covering up for being unable to recall and should be scored as an error. While someone who functions normally may occasionally miss one or two of these test items, several errors almost always indicate a significant problem.

An estimate of severity of the dementia can be made from the number of errors on the Mental Status Questionnaire (Kahn, et al., 1960). Two to five errors indicate mild impairment, five to seven errors suggest moderate impairment, while eight or more errors reflect severe impairment. Errors on similar mental status tests have been found to correlate highly with the amount of brain damage present (Blessed, Tomlinson, & Roth, 1968), with other measures of memory and intellectual impairment (Zarit, Miller, & Kahn, 1978), and with estimates of current functioning, such as ability to dress one's self (Zarit, Reever, & Bach-Peterson, 1980). It should be pointed out, however, that some people function better than their mental status scores might indicate. Thus, this test (or any other) should not be viewed as a substitute for a more complete assessment of the patient's current functioning.

Sometimes the practitioner must consider qualitative differences in errors. A patient who thinks it is 1952 when it is 1985 is more likely to have a serious problem than someone who misses the year by one. Not knowing the date of the month is less significant than being unable to recall the month or year.

People suffering from delirium will also make errors on mental status examinations. While they sometimes respond in similar ways as dementia patients, certain types of errors are much more typical of delirium patients. In contrast to dementia patients who usually try to answer questions, or claim they do not know, a person with delirium will often offer a so-called "symbolic answer." For instance, when asked "Where are you?" someone who calls the nursing home he resides in a "hotel," "resort," or "restaurant," is giving a symbolic answer. These patients may also give even more far-fetched symbolic answers such as reporting having gone on a trip the night before or having been in another facility with the same name, or identifying the interviewer as someone he knew in the past, or as having an entirely different job. Test scores may also fluctuate considerably when the patient suffers from delirium.

In most cases, delirium patients will give answers like those described above. Occasionally a dementia patient will give similar answers, but because symbolic responses are more typical of delirium, their presence indicates the need to investigate for a reversible problem.

A depressed person will often complain of memory loss, as noted earlier, but will usually make no errors on a mental status examination. There are exceptions. A severely depressed individual may not respond at all when tested.

People with head injuries or who have suffered strokes usually have a selective, rather than global impairment of intellect. Some of their abilities are affected and others are not. Mental status testing is inconclusive in evaluating these problems and a more extensive neuropsychological investigation is warranted. For instance, an aphasic patient may score as severely impaired on a mental status examination, because of word-finding problems, but neuropsychological investigations will often indicate abilities which are intact.

Normal persons usually do not make errors on the Mental Status Questionnaire (shown in Table 3.4). It is important, however, to create a relaxed atmosphere and give the patient enough time to answer. The interviewer must also consider the potential effects of hearing loss.

One 82-year-old woman was diagnosed as "hopelessly senile" during a psychiatric hospitalization, and was turned over to her children for care. When they sought information about how to manage her, an assessment revealed she was profoundly deaf. The interviewer then allowed her to read the mental status questions, as well as other memory tests. Performance was normal. By continuing to communicate with her by writing, the interviewer found that the reason for her hospitalization was a grief reaction that followed her husband's death. Neither the circumstances of her hospitalization nor her hearing loss were taken into consideration by the hospital staff, who saw her only as 82 and senile.

A variety of other simple tasks can be used to supplement the mental status questions, including calculations, learning tasks, spelling or counting backwards and similarities (Pfeiffer, 1975; Folstein, Folstein, & McHugh, 1975; Jacobs, Bernhard, Delgado, & Strain, 1977). A particularly reliable procedure is the face-hand test, a measure of the perception of double simultaneous stimulation (Kahn, et al., 1960; Zarit, Miller, & Kahn, 1978). The side of the face and back of the hand are touched simultaneously by the examiner, and the patient is asked where he felt being touched. The test is comprised of 16 face-hand trials, and four trials in which just the face or the hands are stimulated. The pattern of trials is shown in Table 3.5.

TABLE 3.5.
The Face-Hand Test

Instructions: 1. With Eyes Closed: "Please close your eyes. I am going to touch you and I want you to show me where I touched you." (On trials 1–4, if person makes an omission, ask: "Anywhere else?")

2. With Eyes Open: "Now open your eyes. I am going to touch you again. Pay close attention and show me where I touched you."

Test is terminated after either trial 4, 8, 12, or 16, if the patient has completed the preceding four trials correctly.

Circle Omissions; Indicated Displacements with "D"

| Eyes Closed | Eyes Open |
|---|---|
| 1. Right cheek—left hand | 9. Right cheek—left hand |
| 2. Left cheek—right hand | 10. Left cheek—right hand |
| 3. Right cheek—right hand | 11. Right cheek—right hand |
| 4. Left cheek—left hand | 12. Left cheek—left hand |
| Right cheek—left cheek | Right cheek—left cheek |
| Right hand—left hand | Right hand—left hand |
| 5. Right cheek—left hand | 13. Right cheek—left hand |
| 6. Left cheek—right hand | 14. Left cheek—right hand |
| 7. Right cheek—right hand | 15. Right cheek—right hand |
| 8. Left cheek—left hand | 16. Left cheek—left hand |

Scoring: Results suggest brain damage if the patient continues to make errors on the fifth trial or after. Severity of damage is related to the number of errors. Errors before the fifth trial have no clinical significance.

From R. L. Kahn, A. I. Goldfarb, M. Pollack, & A. Peck. Brief objective measures for the determination of mental status in the aged, *American Journal of Psychiatry*, 1960, *117*, 326–328. Copyright 1960 by the American Psychiatric Association. Reprinted by permission.

Testing is stopped after any block of trials is completed correctly. Errors on trial 5 or on subsequent trials raises the possibility of dementia or delirium. Errors on one side of the body only may reflect brain damage. There tend to be few false positive results, but cases of early, mild dementia may go undetected.

**Other Psychological Tests.** There are cases in which symptoms and history have some features which suggest dementia, but mental-status testing indicates no impairment. In these instances, further psychological testing is warranted. Useful instruments include the Wechsler Adult Intelligence Scale (WAIS-R) and the Luria-Nebraska Neuropsychological Battery (Golden, Hammeke, & Purisch, 1978; Golden, et al., 1982). Albert (1981) also describes a neuropsychological approach to dementia.

Results that suggest dementia are obvious deficits in well-learned abilities. For example, if the patient is well educated, low scores on the vocabulary and information subtests of the WAIS-R support a hypothesis of dementia. Low scores on these or other verbal subtests of the WAIS-R are more difficult to evaluate for persons with a high school education or less. Poor performance on nonverbal and timed tasks is typical of normal aging and is not pathognomic for dementia (Zarit, Eiler, & Hassinger, 1985).

In many instances, additional testing will not be sufficient to complete the diagnosis. The problem in identifying early, mild symptoms of dementia is that similar fluctuations in cognitive abilities can be caused by many factors other than dementia. If dementia is present, however, deficiencies in test performance will become more pronounced over time. When the results of an assessment are ambiguous, psychological testing provides a valuable baseline against which future changes can be measured. Retesting at six-month or yearly intervals will clarify whether or not dementia is present. A decline in scores suggests dementia, while stability points to some other explanation for the symptoms. The following case illustrates how retesting clarified diagnosis, and also how important it is not to diagnose dementia in the absence of clear-cut evidence.

Mr. H. is a 66-year-old retired engineer. His wife and daughter reported a gradual onset of memory problems for the past few years, including not remembering events. For instance, he would make a repair at his daughter's house, and then not remember he had done so. Mr. H. confirmed these and other memory problems. He also had a tremor, and had been treated for Parkinson's disease. When he had severe side effects from the anti-Parkinson medications, he sought another medical opinion. The neurologist he saw said he did not have Parkinson's and discontinued the medication, but could not determine the cause of his problems.

During the initial interview, Mr. H. raised one other crucial piece of information. He asked the interviewer if mercury poisoning could be contributing to his problem. He had been using a topical application for several years which contains mercury, and had recently read that prolonged use could be harmful.

Mental status testing was normal, and because of the severity of his presenting problems, it was decided to do the Luria-Nebraska battery to provide additional information. His performance on the Luria-Nebraska was also within normal limits, but there were some weak areas, including tasks involving attention (which accounted for his memory failures) and recognizing tones. Because Mr. H. had an exceptional educational and work history, one would have expected better performance and the test results were interpreted as indicating possible mild cerebral impairment. Coupled with his tremor, the test scores suggested the possibility of mercury poisoning or some other cerebral dysfunction.

As a next step, Mr. H. was referred to a physician for further evaluation. When tests for mercury poisoning proved negative, the physician diagnosed Mr. H. as having early Alzheimer's disease. Our assessment was that neither the history nor testing provided clear-cut evidence of dementia, and it was decided to retest him in six months. If a dementia was present, it would be more apparent by that time.

Retesting on the Luria-Nebraska revealed improved functioning, including the performance on those subtests which had initially been low. Mr. H. and his family also reported improved functioning. Mr. H. clearly did not have Alzheimer's disease. While definitive evidence of mercury poisoning was never obtained, he had stopped the medicine at the time of the initial testing, and had not used it since.

(A summary of the role of testing in assessment of dementia appears in Table 3.2.)

## COORDINATING MEDICAL AND PSYCHOSOCIAL EVALUATIONS

### When to Get a Medical Evaluation

A medical examination is a crucial part of the overall evaluation of someone suspected of having dementia. Whenever there is a possibility that current symptoms may be due to a treatable condition, the person should be referred for a medical evaluation. The circumstances under which a referral should be made include the following.

If someone with memory loss typical of dementia has not previously had a medical examination, the possibility that there is some treatable cause should be investigated.

If a patient has symptoms, history, or test results which suggest a delirium (as described above), then a medical evaluation is crucial. Any indication of delirium, even if it is not consistent, is reason to make a referral.

If there is a sudden worsening in a patient suffering dementia, the possibility exists that there is some treatable problem, and this should be investigated.

## What the Medical Examination Shows

A major conclusion to be drawn from the medical assessment is to rule out all possible treatable causes of dementialike symptoms. As noted previously, there are no medical tests which determine unequivocally that dementia is present, or that one is dealing with a specific type of dementing illness, such as Alzheimer's disease. Physicians can evaluate patients for the many treatable conditions that cause memory loss and similar symptoms. In other words, dementia is a diagnosis of last resort and can only be made after other possible causes have been considered. A proper medical evaluation is described in the article, "Senility Reconsidered" (NIA Task Force, 1980).

One recent diagnostic advance has been the CAT scan or CT scan. This apparatus involves taking multiple X-rays of the brain. It is used to detect many types of abnormalities, including brain tumors and hydrocephalus. Results are more ambiguous in differentiating mild dementia from normal aging. Atrophy of brain matter on a CT scan indicates a possible Alzheimer type of dementia, but many older people with no dementia have some degree of brain atrophy. Evidence of atrophy on a CT scan should never be used to diagnose dementia, without confirming findings from observing other symptoms, history, and testing (NIA Task Force, 1980). Another procedure, the PET scan (Positron Emission Scan) appears promising as a diagnostic tool, but it is still in an experimental stage.

Although no definitive tests exist for differentiating types of dementia, there are some differences in clinical features among the major dementias that make it possible to identify the probable type (see Cummings & Benson, 1983, for a thorough discussion of differences in symptoms among dementing illnesses). Hachinski and his colleagues (Hachinski, Lassen, & Marshall, 1974) have developed a scale for differentiating between Alzheimer's disease and multi-infarct dementia, which has received wide attention. Initial studies suggest that diagnosis using Hachinski's criteria is generally accurate when compared with subsequent autopsy findings (Rosen, Terry, Fuld, Katzman, & Peck, 1980). A recent review, however, has raised several questions about the validity of this approach (Liston & LaRue, 1983). The Hachinski criteria appear in Table 3.6.

Although varying in some symptoms, Alzheimer's disease and multi-infarct dementia may have a similar traumatic impact on the family. In a study which used the Hachinski scoring method to classify cases as either probable Alzheimer's disease or multi-infarct dementia, type of dementia made no difference in the burden on the family, and only small differences in functional problems manifested by the patient (Hassinger, Zarit, & Zarit, 1982).

## CASE EXAMPLES

The assessment principles presented in this chapter will be illustrated by the following examples.

### Case 1. Edna R. / *Age:* 71

Current Symptoms. Information about Mrs. R. was provided by her two daughters. They said Edna forgets how to do simple tasks, such as buttoning clothes. She misplaces things and is unable to cook or shop, although she carries out other household activities. Edna has withdrawn from social contacts and activities. Occasionally, she has trouble finding words.

During an interview, Edna was cooperative and relaxed. Neither she nor her daughters reported symptoms of depression.

TABLE 3.6.
Differentiating Alzheimer's Disease and Multi-Infarct Dementia: The Hachinski
Scoring System

Scores of 4 or less suggest Alzheimer's disease. Seven and above indicate
possible multi-infarct dementia. Between 4 and 7 are mixed or indeterminant
cases.

| Features | Score |
|---|---|
| 1. Abrupt onset | 2 |
| 2. Stepwise deterioration | 1 |
| 3. Fluctuating course | 2 |
| 4. Nocturnal confusion | 1 |
| 5. Relative preservation of personality | 1 |
| 6. Depression | 1 |
| 7. Somatic complaints | 1 |
| 8. Emotional incontinence | 1 |
| 9. History of hypertension | 1 |
| 10. History of strokes | 2 |
| 11. Evidence of associated atherosclerosis | 1 |
| 12. Focal neurological symptoms | 2 |
| 13. Focal neurological signs | 2 |

From V. C. Hachinski, "Differential diagnosis of Alzheimer's dementia: Multi-Infarct
dementia," in B. Reisberg (ed.), *Alzheimer's Disease: The Standard Reference.* (New
York: The Free Press, 1983), p. 188.

**History.** There was gradual onset of memory loss approximately four years earlier. Since then, symptoms gradually worsened, with a sudden exacerbation three months ago when Edna
was hospitalized after a fall. (She suffered a fractured leg in the
fall.)

**Testing.** She was able to answer one question correctly, her
age, on the ten-item Mental Status Questionnaire (see Table 3.7).
While she was cooperative during the testing, she did not try to
guess at the answers. She made errors on the face-hand test with
eyes closed and open.

**Additional Information.** Edna's daughters had brought her
for an evaluation in order to plan how to care for her in the
future. Up until her recent hospitalization, Edna had functioned
independently in her own apartment, receiving help only with

**TABLE 3.7.**
Mental Status Testing for Edna R.

1. Where are you now? (What place is this? What is the name of this place?)
   —I don't know.
2. Where is it located (address)?
   —I don't know.
3. What is the date today?—Day?
   —I don't know.
4. Month?
   —don't know
5. Year?
   —don't know
6. How old are you?
   —71
7. When were you born? Month?
   —I don't know.
8. Year of birth?
   —don't know
9. Who is president of the United States?
   —I don't know.
10. Who was president before him?
    —I don't know.

Additional questions—

Have you ever been in this place before?
—No.
Who am I?
—A doctor.
What do I do? (What's my job called?)
—
Have you ever seen me before?
—No.
Where were you last night?
—At home.

her shopping. Now she had a homemaker who provided 24-hour care during the week. On the weekends, she spent one weekend with one daughter and the next weekend with the other.

Edna made few demands on her daughters or complained to them. She had a thorough medical evaluation three years earlier. At that time, she was pronounced to be suffering from "premature senility", and her daughters were advised to place her in a nursing home, a suggestion they rejected as unnecessary. Her current doctor was supportive of her receiving care at home. When Edna needed tests for a gastrointestinal problem he had advised against hospitalization. At that time, he advised her daughters that it would be much worse for her to remain in the hospital. Her daughters had been skeptical at the time about his advice, but when she had to be hospitalized after her fall, she became quite agitated and difficult to manage. She also was hallucinating, which upset her daughters. These problems ceased after she came home, although her memory remained somewhat worse than before the hospitalization. She was currently taking no medications.

Her daughters wanted to know how to take better care of her. They were especially concerned about how much help to give her when she has trouble doing something around the house. They did not report feeling burdened by the care and supervision they were providing, but they said that other family members call and make them feel guilty for not doing more.

**Discussion.** This case is a straightforward example of a progressive dementia. Symptoms, history, and testing are all consistent with that assessment. Although the earlier medical diagnosis (premature senility) was inexact ("premature" refers to cases with onset between 40 and 55), a thorough investigation for potentially reversible causes had been made. The episode of worsening behavior which occurred at the time of her hospitalization is a typical example of a delirium superimposed upon dementia. Possible causes were the fracture she suffered and the move to an unfamiliar environment. When she returned home, the problems of agitation and hallucinations ceased, but as with many dementia patients who suffer similar upsets, she did not fully regain her previous level of functioning.

It is noteworthy that her physician understood how disruptive hospitalization would be for her, and advised against it at a time before it was necessary. The other interesting feature of the case is the high level of Edna's functioning, despite the test findings of severe impairment that she displayed. One explanation is that she did not try on the tests, as indicated by her "don't know" answers. The score therefore may have been lower than her actual ability. Another possibility is that she had been able to retain her adaptive abilities by staying in a familiar place. Her daughters had been careful not to take away those household tasks she could still perform, even if she could not do them as well as in the past. Their encouragement may have contributed to her functioning fairly well.

**Followup.** Followup with one of her daughters was made a year later. Although Edna continued to decline, the arrangements that the daughters had worked out for supervising her were still adequate. Neither daughter felt overly stressed, and they still reported having positive interactions with her.

### Case 2. Marjorie J. / *Age:* 62

**Current Symptoms.** Marjorie J. was brought to the clinic by her son and daughter, who were concerned about episodes of forgetting that they noticed while she was visiting them. They reported she repeats herself occasionally and forgets where she puts things around the house. Marjorie said she notices these problems and feels embarrassed when they happen, but she wants her children to let her know when she is having trouble. During the interview, Marjorie was mildly anxious and became tearful at a couple of moments.

**History.** Since Marjorie lives in another part of the country, her children have not seen her for several years except for brief visits, and could not provide a clear history. At various points in the interview they reported noticing memory problems two years, five years, and nine years ago. Marjorie also could not tell how long the problem had been going on.

**Testing.** Marjorie made three errors on the Mental Status Questionnaire (see Table 3.8), missing the name of the clinic, its address, and, by one year, her age. She made no errors on the face-hand test. She was also given memory tests from the Luria-

**TABLE 3.8.**
Mental Status Testing for Marjorie J.

1. Where are you now? (What place is this? What is the name of this place?)
   —A medical center. (She did not know the name).
2. Where is it located (address)?
   —(She did not know the address, but knew it was located in Los Angeles, California).
3. What is the date today?—Day?
   —26th (correct)
4. Month?
   —January (correct)
5. Year?
   —1983 (correct)
6. How old are you?
   —63 (incorrect, by one year)
7. When were you born? Month?
   —May
8. Year of birth?
   —1920
9. Who is president of the United States?
   —Reagan
10. Who was president before him?
    —Carter

Additional questions

Have you ever been in this place before?
—No.
Who am I?
—Dr. . . . . I don't remember your name.
What do I do? (What's my job called?)
—

Have you ever seen me before?
—No.
Where were you last night?
—At my daughter's house.

Nebraska Neuropsychological Battery, and made several errors, possibly due to an attention deficit.

**Additional Information.** Her children attributed their mother's problems to their father's overbearing nature. They said he had always dominated their mother, putting her down to build up his ego. Since he retired one year ago, he has taken over all the household activities. Marjorie said, however, that he had been somewhat less dominating in the past year, and was tolerant of her forgetting. He was not available for the interview, having returned already to his home on the East Coast.

Marjorie had a thorough neurological and psychological evaluation during the past year, which failed to reveal any specific cause of her problems. The resulting diagnosis had been "depression" and treatment was recommended. She saw a psychiatrist briefly for psychotherapy, but he had been selected by her husband, and she did not like or trust him. Ultimately, she was prescribed an antidepressant medication, which she takes irregularly.

**Discussion.** Although the memory problems which Marjorie's children describe are consistent with an early dementia, there is not enough information to make a conclusive diagnosis. The history was inadequate, and it was not possible to determine if she had a progressive condition. The errors on her mental status test also are not conclusive. Because Marjorie is from another city, and is not familiar with the hospital where the interview took place, her not knowing its name or address does not represent a significant cognitive deficit. She was able to identify the name of the city and state correctly. More testing would have been desirable, but since she was going home in a few days, it could not be arranged.

Because there was not sufficient evidence of dementia, it was decided to encourage Marjorie to pursue the course recommended to her earlier to receive psychotherapy. She was accordingly referred to a therapist in her community who specialized in treatment of depression. If her memory problems were functional, therapy would potentially ameliorate them. If the problems turned out to be a manifestation of dementia, the therapy still might be useful, as she is aware and concerned about her problem.

The best approach in this case would be to involve her husband. He could provide more information which would be helpful for making an assessment. Marital therapy might then be undertaken if her memory problems did not appear due to dementia. When that possibility was raised during the assessment interview, however, both Marjorie and her children insisted that he would not see a therapist since he did not believe he had any problems.

**Followup.** Followup is critical in this case, in order to clarify diagnosis. If there is further degeneration, then Marjorie's problems would fit a typical dementia pattern. If there is no deterioration or improvement, then we need to look for other explanations of her memory problems, for example, depression or marital conflict.

Followup took place one and one half years after the initial interview. Because Marjorie lives in another city, followup consisted of a telephone interview with her daughter, who had moved back to that city, but was seeing her parents regularly. No testing was done. Her daughter reported that Marjorie continued to have similar problems remembering on occasions, but there had been no worsening and no new problems had developed. Marjorie was described as mildly anxious and depressed. She had gone to the therapist whom she had been referred to, but discontinued after a few visits.

While the etiology of Marjorie's problems still cannot be fully explained, the lack of deterioration suggests that she was not suffering from early symptoms of dementia. This case illustrates the importance of not labelling mild cognitive deficits as dementia. Identifying Marjorie as having dementia or Alzheimer's disease would have had only detrimental effects. For example, it could have confirmed in her husband's eyes that she was not competent.

### Case 3. Harriet T. / *Age:* 66

**Current Symptoms.** Harriet was brought to the clinic by her husband, Bernard, because of his concern about her memory problems. He had been noticing for some time that she could not give correct directions, and she would tell him to turn the wrong way when they were out driving. She had been losing interest in activities, and was sleeping much later than she had in the past. Recently, she misplaced some money and had gotten very concerned about finances. Her housework and cooking were not as good as before, and Bernard was concerned that she was not eating when he was away from home. When the interviewer discussed these problems with Harriet alone, she said that her husband has no confidence in her and treats her like a child. She did not believe she had a memory problem.

**History.** Bernard dated the onset of the problems beginning three years earlier. The first thing he noticed was her giving incorrect directions. New problems gradually appeared since then.

**Testing.** Harriet made no errors on the Mental Status Questionnaire or face-hand test. She reported virtually no depressive symptoms on the Beck Depression Inventory, and had a total score of 2. A WAIS-R was administered, and the results are shown in Table 3.9.

**Additional Information.** Harriet was a well-educated person, holding a master's degree from a prominent university. She had been a leader in her community, including holding elected office, until three years earlier when she began withdrawing from activities.

When seen jointly with her husband, Harriet was quiet and withdrawn, and did not contradict him when he discussed her memory. She became more outgoing, however, when the interviewer saw her alone. It was then that she complained that her husband wanted to be in charge; he tried to tell her what to do. Nonetheless, both she and her husband describe their marriage of 42 years as very rewarding, although it became clear to the interviewer that they are both independent and stubborn.

She had had routine physical examinations, but no workup had been done for her memory problems. Harriet had no known medical problems and was taking no medications. Bernard had

TABLE 3.9.
WAIS-R Scores of Harriet T.

| Subtest | Raw Score | Scaled Score | Age Scaled Score |
|---|---|---|---|
| **Verbal Subtests** | | | |
| Information | 15 | 8 | 9 |
| Digit span | 8 | 5 | 6 |
| Vocabulary | 58 | 12 | 13 |
| Arithmetic | 7 | 6 | 8 |
| Comprehension | 18 | 8 | 10 |
| Similarities | 13 | 6 | 9 |
| **Performance Subtests** | | | |
| Picture completion | 9 | 5 | 8 |
| Picture arrangement | 2 | 4 | 7 |
| Block design | 2 | 3 | 5 |
| Object assembly | 7 | 2 | 4 |
| Digit symbol | 28 | 4 | 9 |

| | Sum of Scaled Scores | IQ |
|---|---|---|
| Verbal | 45 | 94 |
| Performance | 18 | 78 |
| Full scale | 63 | 86 |

suffered a severe heart attack some years earlier, and prided himself on the full recovery he had made, becoming active again as soon as possible. He could not understand why his wife had given up her activities, and believed that to be the cause of her forgetting.

**Discussion.** As in the previous case, the patient's symptoms of memory loss appear at first to be related to conflicts with her husband. Harriet responded quickly on the brief screening tests (Mental Status Questionnaire and face-hand test) and made no errors. However, because of her high education level and the report by her husband of dementialike symptoms, a more complete assessment was made.

The WAIS-R results in Table 3.9 show a pattern consistent with diffuse brain damage. Her scores on both the verbal and performance subtests are far lower than one would expect, given her education and personal achievements. This level of performance could represent normal functioning for an older person with limited education and occupational achievements. The difference between verbal and performance scores is fairly typical in later life. But for Harriet, these scores indicated a serious decline. In cases where the patient has a good educational background, a single administration of the WAIS or other neuropsychological tests reveal dementia-related impairments when there is a major discrepancy between expected and actual scores. It should be noted, however, that depression can also affect cognitive performance, although usually to a lesser degree.

As a result of the test findings, Harriet was referred for a complete medical and neurological examination. No specific cause of her memory symptoms was found, and the presumed etiology was Alzheimer's disease. This was confirmed by the observation of a continued, gradual decline, and by the results of retesting on the screening instruments, which now showed evidence of dementia.

**Followup.** Both Harriet and her husband were followed by a counselor for the purpose of working out, in the context of their marriage, the problems caused by her memory loss. Bernard in fact, now did have to become the one in charge. The counselor also helped him to develop a better understanding of his wife's needs, especially, why she stubbornly denied she was having any problems.

Interestingly, a different picture of their marriage emerged as Bernard understood more about the changes occurring in his wife. Rather than presenting himself as needing to be in charge, he indicated that his wife had been instrumental in many of his major life decisions, and he strongly felt the loss of her guidance. The realization that she could no longer be a confidant was very upsetting.

Ultimately, counseling sessions with Harriet provided her with emotional support. However, she was unable to remember enough from week to week for there to be any consistent followup of issues she raised in the counseling.

## Case 4. Anita G. / *Age:* 70

**Current Symptoms.** Anita G. was brought to the clinic by her husband and daughter, who complained that she was accusing her husband of having an affair with a teenage girl. Her husband, Tony G., is a devout Catholic, and was very upset at the accusations. He denied that he was having an affair and could not understand why reasoning with his wife did not change her mind. Tony and his daughter also reported that Anita's symptoms were worse in the evening and when she was stressed.

When seen alone, Anita said that her husband would sneak out at night after she was asleep to see this girl. She complained that the girl kept her awake at night by whistling. She does not know the girl's name and had not noticed her before her husband started the affair. She also said that the girl comes into their apartment, but runs away when she hears Anita coming. As for her daughter's part in this matter, Anita stated that her daughter has always been a "daddy's girl," and was siding with him. She did not report actually seeing the girl; but she insisted the girl was real.

**History.** Four months earlier, Anita had surgery for a joint replacement because of her severe arthritis. During the recovery period, she began hallucinating, including seeing imagined intruders. These problems subsided after three weeks. About three weeks before she was brought to the clinic, she first began complaining about her husband's affair. She was taking one medication for her arthritis, disalcid, which she had begun after her hospitalization. There was no prior history of memory problems, paranoid symptoms, or other psychiatric problems.

**Testing.** Anita made three errors on the Mental Status Questionnaire (see Table 3.10). She also made errors on the face-hand test with eyes closed and open.

**Other Information.** In cases where complaints of a paranoid nature are expressed, it is important for the practitioner to

**TABLE 3.10.**
Mental Status Testing for Anita G.

1. Where are you now? (What place is this? What is the name of this place?)
   —A place where you try to help people.
2. Where is it located (address)?
   —South Lake Street, in the Wilshire area. (correct)
3. What is the date today?—Day?
   —13th (correct)
4. Month?
   —July (correct)
5. Year?
   —1983 (correct)
6. How old are you?
   —71 (incorrect)
7. When were you born? Month?
   —September (correct)
8. Year of birth?
   —1912 (correct)
9. Who is president of the United States?
   —Reagan
10. Who was president before him?
    —don't know

Additional questions

Have you ever been in this place before?
—No.
Who am I?
—I don't know.
What do I do? (What's my job called?)
—No one told me.
Have you ever seen me before?
—No, I don't think so.
Where were you last night?
—At home.

determine that the statements are false before making a psychiatric diagnosis. In this instance, Tony's denial was confirmed by his daughter. Furthermore, many of the details Anita described were not plausible, such as the girl slipping in and out of the apartment without being seen. Tony reported having been faithful to his wife throughout their marriage.

In addition to her other medical problems, Anita had gradually lost a major portion of her vision due to macular degeneration.

Her visual functioning was especially poor under conditions of reduced illumination.

**Discussion.** Because the onset of symptoms was recent and coincided with major stresses (surgery for the first episode, the introduction of a new medicine for the second), the first possibility to consider is a delirium. The primary symptom of an imagined intruder who is having an affair with her husband can be associated with a delirium, but similar symptoms can be present with dementia or paranoid disorders in late life. Her MSQ and face-hand errors point to an organic cause, though no strong evidence of delirium was noted.

The first step in the intervention was to consult with the doctor treating Anita's arthritis. Her medication, disalcid, is a nonsteroid, anti-inflamatory agent, which is in a class of medications that recently have been reported to contribute to bring about confusional states (Goodwin & Regan, 1982). The physician agreed to withdraw her from the medication on a trial basis and to use other medications for her arthritis. With the change in medications, Anita's suspicions gradually decreased. Although they never disappeared totally, she said she felt he had broken off the affair.

The family was followed by the counselor over time. He did not observe any dementialike deterioration, which was confirmed on retesting. There was one significant flareup of the paranoid symptoms, but that subsided after the G.'s moved from their home into their daughter's, where Anita felt more secure.

In retrospect, Anita appeared to be suffering from a drug-induced delirium, which was possibly compounded by the deterioration of her vision. Another potential contributing factor is the pain from her arthritis. When the drug was discontinued, the symptoms subsided, but reappeared again under stress. Medical evaluations could find no further cause of these symptoms. The continuation of mild paranoid symptoms suggests a late-life paranoid disorder, perhaps related to decreased sensory abilities, although the specific etiology remains unknown. The major implication of the case is that the acute flareup of symptoms was transitory. It was not predictive of a degenerative process.

## Case 5. Cheryl M. / *Age:* 60

**Current Symptoms.** Cheryl M. was very anxious during an initial interview she had made because she was concerned about memory impairment and thought she might have Alzheimer's disease, which she had read about in a health magazine. During the interview, she would begin a sentence and then jump to another thought midway, never completing the first sentence. She reported feeling exhausted and being unable to carry out tasks at home, such as cleaning or paying the bills. She was also concerned that problems concentrating and frequent absences from work were putting her in jeopardy of being fired from her job as a word processor.

**History.** Cheryl initially said her problems had been occurring for the past year when she began feeling "burned out" and unable to function as well as she liked. She then said she had some difficulty with learning new things since she had been in an automobile accident ten years earlier, in which she had suffered a concussion. She had two previous psychiatric hospitalizations at times of stress in her life, once while in college and the second time following the breakup of her marriage. Although the specific reasons for the hospitalizations were not clear, depression seemed prominent each time, according to her retrospective account. She reported struggling with depression most of her life, as the result of feeling rejected by her parents.

**Testing.** She made no errors on the Mental Status Questionnaire or face-hand test. Memory tests from the Luria-Nebraska Neuropsychological Battery were administered and indicated mild problems with attention, but her overall performance was excellent. A WAIS-R was administered and the results, which are shown in Table 3.11, are somewhat lower than might be expected, given her college education. On a Beck Depression Inventory, she scored 23, indicating moderate depression.

**Additional Information.** Cheryl reported that she was sleeping only two or three hours a night. She had to travel al-

TABLE 3.11.
WAIS-R Scores of Cheryl M.

| Subtest | Raw Score | Scaled Score | Age Scaled Score |
|---|---|---|---|
| **Verbal Subtests** | | | |
| Information | 24 | 12 | 13 |
| Digit span | 16 | 10 | 11 |
| Vocabulary | 67 | 16 | 16 |
| Arithmetic | 10 | 8 | 9 |
| Comprehension | 23 | 11 | 11 |
| Similarities | 22 | 11 | 13 |
| **Performance Subtests** | | | |
| Picture completion | 15 | 9 | 11 |
| Picture arrangement | 10 | 7 | 10 |
| Block design | 34 | 10 | 13 |
| Object assembly | 24 | 7 | 9 |
| Digit symbol | 41 | 6 | 9 |

| | Sum of Scaled Scores | IQ |
|---|---|---|
| Verbal | 68 | 113 |
| Performance | 39 | 100 |
| Full scale | 107 | 108 |

most three hours each way by bus to get to work and was concerned that she would oversleep and miss her bus. As a result, she would wake herself up several hours before it was necessary to go to work. About once a week she would be so tired that she would oversleep anyway, and miss work.

**Discussion.** The test results in this case were generally good. The one test with low scores was the WAIS. Her performance was marred by her poor attention, and she lost several points because of her distractibility. Because of the absence of any definite symptoms of dementia, the more prominent problems of anxiety and depression were probable causes of her cognitive complaints. The role of sleep deprivation also needed to be considered.

Treatment for Cheryl's problems was begun using a structured psychotherapy based on Lewinsohn's model of therapy for depression (Lewinsohn, et al., 1978). Although treatment proceeded slowly at first, she began to show marked improvements after the tenth session. The change in her problem occurred after she and her therapist worked out a plan for her to sleep longer. Other efforts to reduce her feelings of depression also began to work. As her depression decreased, so did her complaints about cognitive impairment. Her work performance also improved markedly. Followups two years after the initial appointment indicated no recurrence of cognitive symptoms or of her depression.

In summary, Cheryl's cognitive complaints were related to anxiety and depression, and perhaps also to mild sleep deprivation. Treatment of these problems resulted in substantial improvements in all areas of her life, including cognitive performance. The absence of a significant cognitive deficit in the initial testing pointed toward depression and away from dementia.

## SUMMARY

Making an adequate and accurate assessment of the differences among senile dementia, delirium, reversible dementia, other types of brain damage, and depression are subtle and can be confusing. The assessment will be difficult, and will take time. Overall, however, it is best to err on the side of pursuing treatable causes, until all the possibilities are exhausted. Clearly, it is very worthwhile to seek out second opinions, if some questions about the potential reversibility of symptoms have not, as yet, been addressed. Before planning any therapeutic interventions, it is essential to determine that dementia is present, to the best of the practitioner's ability.

# CHAPTER 4

# UNDERSTANDING THE STRESS OF CAREGIVERS: PLANNING AN INTERVENTION

Few other disorders place so much stress on family members as dementia. Caregivers routinely report stress-related symptoms, such as anxiety, depression, or feelings of fatigue. They are often angry or resentful, feel guilty about not doing enough, even though they may spend 24 hours a day with the patient. The stresses they experience have many sources. Often they must take over tasks that the patient can no longer do, such as housekeeping or dressing the patient. They must keep vigilant watch over the patient; and often must cope with the patient's specific behavioral disturbances, such as wandering around or not sleeping at night. Moreover, caregivers often experience a great sense of personal and psychological loss as they see their relative gradually decline. Often, the care they must provide demands all of their time. They usually get little relief from the daily strain. They even may be criticized by other relatives.

While the current treatments for dementia patients cannot alleviate the primary medical problems that plague the patient and family, there are procedures which can modify the stress experienced by family members. This chapter will identify the sources of stress on them, and subsequent chapters will discuss possible interventions.

To understand how the patient's symptoms place stress on the family, it is important to consider two propositions. First, diagnosis is only the starting point in treatment planning. Once it is determined that the patient has dementia, other information must be obtained to identify what specific impairments in everyday functioning are present. Because dementias vary in their symptoms and course, it is difficult to determine from the diagnosis alone when problems will arise. Similarly, caregivers do not all find the same problems stressful. Some report a lot of stress associated with specific behaviors, while others report the contrary. The task for the practitioner, then, is to obtain specific information about what problems the patient is having in everyday life, and how the caregiver will react to those problems, in order to identify the areas in which the caregiver may need help. The second proposition is that the burden or stress on family members is determined by several factors, such as the caregiver's skills in coping with difficult or problem behavior and by the social support provided by other family members. Some of the burden might be alleviated. A key to making successful interventions is to identify the specific sources of the burden present in a given case and the extent to which it may be alleviated.

## GOING BEYOND DIAGNOSIS

The diagnostic process is the crucial first step for assisting families in which there may be a troubled member. It establishes the presence or absence of a dementing illness in this individual. For many medical problems the diagnosis points to a particular course of treatment. In the case of senile dementia, however, the situation is different. Here, interventions are focused on the management of problem behaviors, and other stresses of caregiving. The problems encountered vary considerably from one patient to another, as do the possibilities for dealing with them. Therefore, it is necessary to make an individualized assessment of the patient's behavior and its impact on the caregiver and other family members.

Individual variation in symptoms among dementia patients is great. While the brain damage associated with dementia is progressive, behaviors change at different rates and problems vary among patients. One person may have trouble dressing himself in the early stages of the disease, while another will have no problems in dressing, even when the brain damage is severe. Even in a more physiological area, incontinence, patient response will vary widely. It is often assumed that dementia patients will eventually become incontinent, but incontinence can be associated with many treatable problems, for example, medications, bladder infections, or the inability to find the bathroom. Some dementia patients never become incontinent.

Studies of the effects of brain damage caused by dementing illnesses on behavior confirm the variability of symptoms among patients (Blessed, Tomlinson, & Roth, 1968). Although the numbers of problems increase with severity of brain damage, there is no one-to-one correspondence between problems and amount of damage. Many factors mediate the occurrence and the effect of physical deficits. Motivation, education, work history, environmental condition, as well as the patient's and family's reactions to the disease, all influence the way in which deficits are manifested (Kahn & Miller, 1978).

It is also important to note that some problems will worsen as the disease progresses, but others will get better. For example, a woman may at one point in the disease insist on preparing meals independently, despite obvious need of assistance. Later on, however, she may be more willing to accept assistance. Patients may struggle to remain independent, making it difficult for the family to provide assistance or supervision, but this problem often diminishes over time. In addition, paranoid reactions and wandering can also decrease over time.

Overall, dementia needs to be viewed as a disease in which functional problems will vary considerably from case to case. Similarly, families reactions vary tremendously. The clinician should not assume that particular psychological conflicts or dynamics are always present. Rather, he must be careful and systematic to understand the caregiver's reaction, so as to learn about the unique resources and deficits in each particular family.

## Determinants of Burden

Service providers should never assume how much stress a family is under, just because dementia has been diagnosed or the patient has certain symptoms. It is often assumed that families caring for a dementia patient at home will come to the point when they cannot cope with their relative when the disease progresses to a particular level of severity, for instance, when a patient becomes incontinent or has problems with dressing, bathing or feeding oneself. However, both research and clinical experience indicate considerable variability among families. Some report feeling very high levels of stress, even though the patient has very few behavioral problems. Others cope with the most severe changes, but report little stress. Overall, severity of behavioral and cognitive symptoms has not been found to be a good indication of how much burden or stress caregivers are experiencing (Zarit, Reever, & Bach-Peterson, 1980; J. Zarit, 1982).

It may seem surprising that the severity of the disease does not necessarily correlate with the degree of burden experienced, but other factors associated with burden should be considered. The most important predictors of the caregiver's degree of burden have been found to include how the caregiver manages memory and behavior problems; the social support available to the caregiver; and the quality of the relationship between the patient and caregiver before the onset of the disease. With respect to managing problems, when the caregiver is flexible and tries out new approaches, the burden tends to be experienced as less stressful. Caregivers who persist in responding to the patient as if he/she was not brain damaged are often frustrated and report a great deal of stress. They fail to recognize that the patient *cannot* respond as before the brain damage occurred. Social support is also critical in determining the amount of stress families may have to endure. When more family members are involved in the care of the dementia patient, and when the primary caregiver perceives the family or other helpers as supportive, the caregiver may not feel as burdened. Quality of the relationship between the patient and caregiver prior to the disease also affects the amount of stress caregivers will experience. As would be expected, caregivers who report a better relationship in the past will face current problems with less stress. Factors associated with burden are summarized in Figure 4.1.

The extent of burden can be modified; for instance, if caregivers change how they cope with problem behavior or receive more social support. By assessing the particular factors contributing to the caregivers distress in a given case, the practitioner will have a better idea of how to intervene to lessen the sense of burden.

## ASSESSING THE STRESS ON CAREGIVERS

In order to understand the stresses that the patient places on a particular caregiver, it is important to determine the following: the patient's current memory and behavior problems; the family's reactions to those problems; the social supports available to the family; and the amount of burden on the primary caregiver. Another important assessment is to find out what help the family is asking for. These assessments provide the information necessary for making the types of interventions discussed in subsequent chapters which can lower the burden on caregivers.

**FIGURE 4.1**
Determinants of Caregiver's Burden

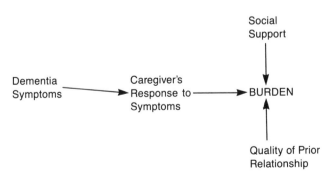

## Assessing Memory and Behavior Problems

The patient's memory and behavior problems can typically be assessed in a straightforward way by questioning the caregiver or other people who interact regularly with the patient. Caregivers usually will report current problems spontaneously, and the interviewer can then ask about other problems that may be occurring.

Some caregivers can give a lot of information about current problems and their frequency. Others, however, give only a few impressions. In those instances, the interviewer must work to gain more specific information. When the practitioner can get concrete information about what problems are occurring and how often, the situation may seem less severe than the caregiver initially described it. In contrast, people under stress are often vague about what is happening and exaggerate events all out of proportion. When that is the case, the first step is to help caregivers overcome the sense of facing an overwhelming and uncontrollable situation. Teaching them to be more specific in identifying the patient's current problems often contributes to this goal.

Occasionally, a caregiver responds to an interviewer's questions about memory and behavior problems by getting worried and asking if his relative will eventually have those problems. This situation is best handled by responding that there are large individual differences among patients, and stressing to caregivers that their relative may or may not develop these problems. The caregiver can also be encouraged to look at how current problems can be managed better, rather than worrying about the future. If caregivers learn to manage current problems better, they are developing skills that may help them with subsequent problems.

After the interviewer has established the occurrence of a particular memory or behavior problem, the next step is to assess the reaction of the caregiver to it. As can be expected, there is considerable variation in how caregivers react to specific problems. For example, clinical experience has shown that caregivers will respond quite differently to repetitive questions by the patient.

Usually, dementia patients repeat questions for one of two reasons. Either their short-term memory is so impaired that they cannot remember asking the question and hearing the answer, or they are attempting to have some sort of social interaction with the family, but they are no longer able to initiate conversations in more appropriate ways.

Many caregivers express great distress when their relative asks the same question over and over. They interpret the patient's behavior as intentional. For example, some caregivers have reacted, "He isn't trying to remember," or "He does it to annoy me." Yet caregivers who understand that the repetitiveness is not intentional are more apt to develop a positive method to handle it and not to feel as distressed by it. Similarly, with a problem as disturbing as incontinence, not all caregivers are upset to the same degree. One man became extremely distraught over taking over the household finances when his wife was unable to continue to handle them. Yet after the disease progressed, he had little difficulty coping with his wife's incontinence. Clearly, to understand the impact of symptoms on the caregiver, it is important to know how the caregiver reacts.

There are two dimensions to examine in relation to a caregiver's reaction to specific problems. The first is the subjective reality of how a behavior will affect the relationship between the caregiver and patient. As we have seen, some problems will be more significant to caregivers. For example, some report great distress by the demands placed on them to take over more responsibility in supervising and caring for the patient. Others are more embarrased if the patient cannot maintain appropriate responses in social situations, such as carrying on a conversation with friends or using appropriate table manners in a restaurant. Some caregivers may feel mortified if the patient repeats himself in conversation. Others are bothered most by the changes in the person they once knew—the patient is no longer a friend and confidant. Another factor affecting caregivers' subjective reactions has to do with whether they see the behavior problem as intentional or not, as in the example of repetitive questions discussed above. Overall, it is important to understand that caregivers vary in their reactions to problem behaviors, depending on the significance the disability has for them. Possible solutions to overcome stress may become apparent to the practitioner or caregiver, once the meaning that the patient's problems have for the caregiver can be identified.

The second factor which determines caregivers' reactions to the aberrant behavior of a relative is the problem-solving strategies they use. Caregivers who are able to apply effective problem-solving strategies in response to altered behavior generally report less stress or burden than those who use ineffective methods. Here, problem solving can be described as a process which provides strategies for the development of optimal means to manage stressors, in this case, the patient's altered behavior. Successful problem solving might include identifying situations which trigger problem behavior, developing new responses to the patient to minimize the effects of the impaired behavior, and seeking assistance from others when caregiving tasks become excessive. For example, if the patient begins to have trouble getting dressed, some caregivers will look at the situation to figure out what changes *they* can make to assist the patient. They may determine that the patient cannot follow a complex sequence. Saying to the patient, "Go to your room and get dressed," does not work, because the patient has forgotten the second part of the command before getting to the bedroom. By trial and error, the caregiver discovers that the patient can follow the direction, "Get dressed" if it is given when the patient is already in the bedroom. Or it may be necessary to break the task of dressing into small steps and to give a directive at each step. It may also be helpful for some caregivers to bring in another person to assist with the dressing, if it has become difficult for the afflicted person to dress himself. In summary, solving the problems of difficult behavior involves analyzing the problem and learning to manage the disruption it causes.

It is important to note that inadequate problem solving and the resulting inappropriate responses can actually increase the stress on the caregiver, and sometimes also on the patient. Some maladaptive responses include insisting that the patient has to behave "normally," even though he is unable to do so; to become overwhelmed by even small problems; hoping that someone else will step in with a magical or perfect solution to the problem or with a cure for the patient; or feeling excessively guilty or responsible for having caused the dementia.

The examples described above show that the meaning caregivers give to a problem behavior and their response to it are interrelated. Some interpretations of the meaning for behavior are more likely to lead to effective problem solving and successful means to deal with a patient, while others generally lead to less effective or poor coping responses. As was noted before, the caregiver who believes the patient asks repetitive questions intentionally is less likely to make a positive, successful response than the caregiver who understands the behavior is not intentional.

The Memory and Behavior Problems Checklist, shown in Table 4.1, has been developed to determine the frequency of current problems and how caregivers react to them. This instrument can be given to caregivers to supplement information obtained from an interview, or the practitioner can use it as a guideline for asking questions during an interview about what functions are most likely affected by dementia. We would not recommend handing the Memory and Behavior Problems Checklist to clients to fill out. Rather, it should be used with other methods of evaluation, such as a structured interview after some rapport has been developed. As a research tool, this instrument has been found to have adequate reliability and validity (J. Zarit, 1982).

## Assessing Social Supports

Social support has two components, one relating to the patient and the other to the caregiver. The first is a physical or instrumental component, which includes activities such as assistance with bathing, cleaning, cooking, and the tasks involved in day-to-day care. The second component is an emotional one that provides the feeling of support gained from knowing that there is someone who understands the caregiver's experience and offers encouragement in times of difficulty. Support can be infor-

**TABLE 4.1.**
Memory and Behavior Problems Checklist

**INSTRUCTIONS TO INTERVIEWER**
This checklist has two parts. Part A measures the frequency with which problems occur. Part B determines to what degree the behavior upsets the caregiver. Begin by asking if a problem has occurred and, if so, how often. When you find it has occurred, then go immediately to Part B, and determine the caregiver's reaction to that problem *when it occurs*. (In other words, do not go through the whole list for frequency, and then come back to get their reaction.)

**Instructions to Caregiver**
Part A. "I am going to read you a list of common problems. Tell me if any of these problems have occurred during the past week. If so how often have they occurred? If not, has this problem ever occurred?" Hand the subject the card on which the frequency and reaction ratings are printed.

Part B. "How much does this problem bother or upset you at the time it happens. The subject indicates his/her typical reaction on the card on which the frequency and reaction ratings are printed. Reaction is how the person reacts when the problem occurs. When the caregiver's response to frequency is "7," you determine reaction by asking:

"How much does it bother or upset you when you have to supervise N to prevent that?"

**FREQUENCY RATINGS**

0 = never occurred
1 = has occurred, but not
    in past week
2 = has occurred 1 or 2 times
    in past week
3 = has occurred 3 to 6 times
    in past week
4 = occurs daily or more often
7 = would occur, if not
    supervised by caregiver
    (eg., wandering except door
    is locked).
8 = patient never performed
    this activity

**REACTION RATINGS:** How much does this bother or upset you when it happens?

0 = not at all
1 = a little
2 = moderately
3 = very much
4 = extremely

| BEHAVIORS | FREQUENCY | REACTION |
|---|---|---|
| 1. Wandering or getting lost | 0  1  2  3  4  7 | 0  1  2  3  4 |
| 2. Asking the same question over and over again | 0  1  2  3  4 | 0  1  2  3  4 |
| 3. Hiding things (money, jewelry, etc) | 0  1  2  3  4 | 0  1  2  3  4 |
| 4. Being suspicious or accusative | 0  1  2  3  4 | 0  1  2  3  4 |

78

**TABLE 4.1.** (Continued)

| BEHAVIORS | FREQUENCY | REACTION |
|---|---|---|
| 5. Losing or misplacing things | 0 1 2 3 4 | 0 1 2 3 4 |
| 6. Not recognizing familiar people | 0 1 2 3 4 | 0 1 2 3 4 |
| 7. Forgetting what day it is | 0 1 2 3 4 | 0 1 2 3 4 |
| 8. Starting, but not finishing things | 0 1 2 3 4 | 0 1 2 3 4 |
| 9. Destroying property | 0 1 2 3 4 | 0 1 2 3 4 |
| 10. Doing things that embarrass you | 0 1 2 3 4 | 0 1 2 3 4 |
| 11. Waking you up at night | 0 1 2 3 4 | 0 1 2 3 4 |
| 12. Being constantly restless | 0 1 2 3 4 | 0 1 2 3 4 |
| 13. Being constantly talkative | 0 1 2 3 4 | 0 1 2 3 4 |
| 14. Talking little or not at all | 0 1 2 3 4 | 0 1 2 3 4 |
| 15. Engaging in behavior that is potentially dangerous to others or self | 0 1 2 3 4 7 | 0 1 2 3 4 |
| 16. Reliving situations from the past | 0 1 2 3 4 | 0 1 2 3 4 |
| 17. Seeing or hearing things that are not there (hallucinations or illusions) | 0 1 2 3 4 | 0 1 2 3 4 |
| 18. Unable or unwilling to dress self (either partly or totally, or inappropriate dress compared to previous standards) | 0 1 2 3 4 7 | 0 1 2 3 4 |
| 19. Unable or unwilling to feed self | 0 1 2 3 4 7 | 0 1 2 3 4 |
| 20. Unable or unwilling to bathe or shower by self | 0 1 2 3 4 7 | 0 1 2 3 4 |
| 21. Unable to put on make-up or shave by self | 0 1 2 3 4 7 | 0 1 2 3 4 |
| 22. Incontinent of bowel or bladder | 0 1 2 3 4 7 | 0 1 2 3 4 |
| 23. Unable to prepare meals | 0 1 2 3 4 7 8 | 0 1 2 3 4 |
| 24. Unable to use the phone | 0 1 2 3 4 7 | 0 1 2 3 4 |
| 25. Unable to handle money (e.g., to complete a transaction in a store; do not include being unable to manage finances) | 0 1 2 3 4 7 | 0 1 2 3 4 |
| 26. Unable to clean house | 0 1 2 3 4 7 8 | 0 1 2 3 4 |
| 27. Unable to shop (to pick out adequate or appropriate foods) | 0 1 2 3 4 7 8 | 0 1 2 3 4 |
| 28. Unable to do other simple tasks which he/she used to do (e.g., put away groceries, simple repairs) | 0 1 2 3 4 7 | 0 1 2 3 4 |
| 29. Unable to stay alone by self | 0 1 2 3 4 | 0 1 2 3 4 |
| 30. Are there any other problems? | 0 1 2 3 4 | 0 1 2 3 4 |

mal, coming from family members, friends, and neighbors, or formal, provided by social-service or health agencies or a counselor or support group.

Research has shown that caregivers who receive calls and visits from family members feel less burdened than those who do not (Zarit, Reever, & Bach-Peterson, 1980). There is a tendency for caregivers to become quite isolated, receiving fewer and fewer visits from friends and going out less. This can be the result of the dementia patient's inappropriate social behavior and/or the caregiver's sensitivity to how others might react to the behavior changes brought about by the disease. This decrease in social contact may be the single most stressful element in caregiving because it cuts the caregiver off from stabilizing normal interactions with other people. And, of course, the lack of social support is believed to be one of many interacting variables involved in greater risk of emotional and physical illness.

Caretakers often request someone to stay with the dementia patient or to take the patient out so the caregivers themselves can gain respite from the continual demands and pressures the patient places on them. They also may need someone to help with shopping, cooking, cleaning, or bathing the patient. In a study comparing husbands and wives as caregivers, it was found that husbands were significantly more likely to have paid help working in the home (J. Zarit, 1982). Women seem more likely to take on the entire responsibility of caregiving and are more reluctant to ask for help. Many of our clients "protected" other family members from knowing the extent of impairment of the patient, either because they did not want to burden others or because of embarrassment over the behavior. In their efforts to protect others, these caregivers actually increase their own burden which diminishes their effectiveness, as we have pointed out. The timely use of homemakers and day-care can considerably reduce stress for the caregiver and delay premature institutionalization of the affected person.

Emotional support is a complex issue for someone caring for a disturbed relative. Phone calls and visits from family members and friends most certainly communicate their continued involvement with and support (usually) the caregiver. But it would be incorrect to assume that all such contacts are positive. Consider the case of a man who has made a vow to himself that he will care for his wife at home no matter how impaired she becomes. But his children call him almost daily urging him to institutionalize her. These calls are hardly supportive; in fact, they are likely to add to his distress.

In assessing relationships within the family and with friends it is important to determine how supportive they actually are. In some situations, the caregiver will be fortunate enough to have someone to talk to when upset or troubled. Some families have a member who serves in this role, but in many families there is not a history of confiding in one another. A counselor or support group might take on this role.

When determining the support the caregiver currently receives, it is wise for counselors to consider strengths and weaknesses in order to tailor an intervention to each case. Table 4.2 summarizes the most common types of social support available. However, not all caregivers need to use all types of support. The simplest way to find out what are the best kinds of help to provide is to ask the caregiver whether a particular service would be helpful.

## Assessing the Caregiver's Burden

The burden of caregiving can be emotional and physical, as well as financial. Through careful questioning, the practitioner can determine if there has been an increase in emotional and physical demands and if there are financial problems. Is the caregiver feeling anxious, depressed, socially isolated or pre-occupied with money issues? How often are these feelings aroused and what events seem to trigger them? Is the caregiver experiencing more medical problems? What are the caregiver's financial concerns and financial situation? Nonverbal cues about stress, anxiety, or depression are important and should be followed up with questions. Crying frequently, not sleeping well, loss of appetite, fatigue, and changes in activities are all important signs that the caregiver is undergoing great stress.

TABLE 4.2.
Types of Social Support

| | |
|---|---|
| Physical tasks: | Bathing |
| | Dressing |
| | Cooking |
| | Dispensing medications and other medical care |
| | Cleaning |
| | Shopping |
| | Sitting or supervising |
| | Activities for the patient (e.g., exercise) |
| | Day care |
| | Transportation |
| | Overnight respite |
| | |
| Emotional tasks: | Someone who understands what the caregiver is experiencing |
| | Someone to talk to when troubled or upset |
| | Someone who will call the caregiver |
| | Someone the caregiver can call at any time |
| | Someone who will give the caregiver encouragement |

In rare instances, the caregiver may express suicidal or homicidal thoughts. In this situation, the practitioner has the responsibility to determine the degree of seriousness of the threat. If the practitioner has no experience dealing with crisis intervention, he or she should immediately refer the patient to an appropriate professional. While often difficult to determine, a standard evaluation includes asking if the person has an actual plan for the suicide or homicide and a means to carry out the plan. Someone who says she has thought of taking pills to end her life but has no potentially lethal medications in the house is less likely to do so than someone who has the intent *and* the means. The interviewer also should attempt to determine if the caregiver has set a date by which the plan is to be carried out. It can also help to ask if anything has kept them from carrying out the plan.

Needless to say, a suicidal or homicidal thought is serious if the caregiver has a plan and the means to carry it out, and is actively considering doing so in the near future. If this occurs, the practitioner must try to establish an agreement with the caregiver that ensures he or she will not carry out the act before the next appointment. This is often difficult to accomplish, especially if the interviewer is not well acquainted with the caregiver. If this assurance is not forthcoming, the practitioner needs to take the steps appropriate to protect the caregiver and/or intended victim. Depending on the situation, these steps might include arranging for a psychiatric evaluation, police intervention, and notifying an intended victim. Once again practitioners who do not feel competent or comfortable responding to a suicidal or homicidal client should immediately refer that person to an appropriate professional.

The Burden Interview, shown in Table 4.3, has been developed to evaluate the subjective impact of caregiving (Zarit, Reever, & Bach-Peterson, 1980; J. Zarit, 1982). It has been used primarily in research and norms have not been developed as yet to indicate mild, moderate, or severe degrees of burden. Preliminary findings, however, suggest this instrument taps important dimensions of the stress experienced by caregivers. Practitioners may find some or all of the questions useful to ask the caregiver as a way of estimating how much stress he or she is currently experiencing. If the extent of the burden on the caregiver has been assessed before an intervention, then administering the Burden Interview again after the intervention will indicate the degree of success or improvement in the caregiver's situation.

### What the Family Is Asking For

The most important factor in deciding the direction of intervention is what help family members want for themselves and the patient. There are two errors practitioners can make in assessing the family's preferences. The first error is to decide that, as a practitioner, you know what would be best for the family, and to tell them what to do, without considering their needs or wishes. The second error is to assume that families have enough information when they seek help to decide what they want. The best way to elicit the family's preferences is to discuss various alternatives and to allow decisions to come out of dialog, in which the practitioner learns about a family's situation and the family, in turn, becomes more knowledgeable about dementia and the alternatives for dealing with it.

**TABLE 4.3.**

The Burden Interview
_____

**INSTRUCTIONS:**

The following is a list of statements, which reflect how people sometimes feel when taking care of another person. After each statement, indicate how often you feel that way, never, rarely, sometimes, quite frequently, or nearly always. There are no right or wrong answers.

1. Do you feel that your relative asks for more help than he/she needs?
   0. Never 1. Rarely 2. Sometimes 3. Quite Frequently 4. Nearly Always
2. Do you feel that because of the time you spend with your relative that you don't have enough time for yourself?
   0. Never 1. Rarely 2. Sometimes 3. Quite Frequently 4. Nearly Always
3. Do you feel stressed between caring for your relative and trying to meet other responsibilities for your family or work?
   0. Never 1. Rarely 2. Sometimes 3. Quite Frequently 4. Nearly Always
4. Do you feel embarrassed over your relative's behavior?
   0. Never 1. Rarely 2. Sometimes 3. Quite Frequently 4. Nearly Always
5. Do you feel angry when you are around your relative?
   0. Never 1. Rarely 2. Sometimes 3. Quite Frequently 4. Nearly Always
6. Do you feel that your relative currently affects your relationship with other family members or friends in a negative way?
   0. Never 1. Rarely 2. Sometimes 3. Quite Frequently 4. Nearly Always
7. Are you afraid what the future holds for your relative?
   0. Never 1. Rarely 2. Sometimes 3. Quite Frequently 4. Nearly Always
8. Do you feel your relative is dependent upon you?
   0. Never 1. Rarely 2. Sometimes 3. Quite Frequently 4. Nearly Always
9. Do you feel strained when you are around your relative?
   0. Never 1. Rarely 2. Sometimes 3. Quite Frequently 4. Nearly Always
10. Do you feel your health has suffered because of your involvement with your relative?
    0. Never 1. Rarely 2. Sometimes 3. Quite Frequently 4. Nearly Always
11. Do you feel that you don't have as much privacy as you would like because of your relative?
    0. Never 1. Rarely 2. Sometimes 3. Quite Frequently 4. Nearly Always
12. Do you feel that your social life has suffered because you are caring for your relative?
    0. Never 1. Rarely 2. Sometimes 3. Quite Frequently 4. Nearly Always
13. Do you feel uncomfortable about having friends over because of your relative?
    0. Never 1. Rarely 2. Sometimes 3. Quite Frequently 4. Nearly Always
14. Do you feel that your relative seems to expect you to take care of him/her, as if you were the only one he/she could depend on?
    0. Never 1. Rarely 2. Sometimes 3. Quite Frequently 4. Nearly Always
15. Do you feel that you don't have enough money to care for your relative, in addition to the rest of your expenses?
    0. Never 1. Rarely 2. Sometimes 3. Quite Frequently 4. Nearly Always
16. Do you feel that you will be unable to take care of your relative much longer?
    0. Never 1. Rarely 2. Sometimes 3. Quite Frequently 4. Nearly Always

**TABLE 4.3.** (Continued)

---

17. Do you feel you have lost control of your life since your relative's illness?
    0. Never 1. Rarely 2. Sometimes 3. Quite Frequently 4. Nearly Always
18. Do you wish you could just leave the care of your relative to someone else?
    0. Never 1. Rarely 2. Sometimes 3. Quite Frequently 4. Nearly Always
19. Do you feel uncertain about what to do about your relative?
    0. Never 1. Rarely 2. Sometimes 3. Quite Frequently 4. Nearly Always
20. Do you feel you should be doing more for your relative?
    0. Never 1. Rarely 2. Sometimes 3. Quite Frequently 4. Nearly Always
21. Do you feel you could do a better job in caring for your relative?
    0. Never 1. Rarely 2. Sometimes 3. Quite Frequently 4. Nearly Always
22. Overall, how burdened do you feel in caring for your relative?
    0. Never 1. Rarely 2. Sometimes 3. Quite Frequently 4. Nearly Always

Modified from J. Zarit, 1982. Copyright © 1983 by Steven H. Zarit and Judy Maes Zarit.

Very few families come to an agency knowing what they want. They often have been given fragmented bits of information and advice. They may have been given different opinions on what to do. For instance, a spouse caring for her husband might have been told by the doctor to put him in a nursing home, while her daughter might suggest that he is not so sick and she should keep him at home. The advantages and disadvantages of neither of these alternatives have been explained to her (much less what the implications of the disease are). In helping families decide what they want, the practitioner begins by finding out what they already know or have been told and how they have tried to deal with the problem. Then the practitioner can present information about possible strategies which they might use to alter or augment them.

Even when a family says that they know what they want, it is best to take some time to explore with them what they have been told, what they have considered, and what they have tried. There may be alternatives they are not aware of.

One family came to our clinic saying they had to put their relative in a nursing home. There were several family members assisting in his care, primarily the patient's sister and nephew, but others also helped out at times. They initially felt that the burden on the sister was too great, especially since the nephew had just taken on new job responsibilities and could not help as much. For that reason, they felt they had to put him in a nursing home. When asked what else they had considered besides a nursing home, they did not think there were other alternatives. When they were told about the possibility of arranging for in-home help, they were interested in trying that instead of nursing home care. They were also encouraged to investigate nursing homes, and when they did, they realized the quality of care was not as good as they expected. They hired a homemaker to take over some responsibilities from the sister, and found that eased her burden.

## SUMMARY

In order to understand the stress on families of dementia patients and to plan to relieve it, the practitioner must gather accurate information about the problems and resources of the particular family and patient in question. Generalized ideas about stages of dementia, preconceived notions about family dynamics, or a set concept about what is best for families, can be misleading. Behavior varies to too great an extent, as do the values and resources of families to apply one approach as the "right" one. Rather, practitioners must take each case on its own merit and assess relevant clinical dimensions, including the problem behaviors currently present, the caregiver's reactions to them, social support available to the caregiver, current stress or burden on the caregiver, and the family's values and preferences.

# CHAPTER 5

# INTERVENTIONS FOR FAMILIES OF DEMENTIA PATIENTS: A STRESS-MANAGEMENT MODEL

To effectively help a caregiver, the practitioner should have a clear understanding of the nature of the stress the person is experiencing, the means to ease the burden, and the likely outcome of the intervention. The approach to helping the caregiver described in this chapter is based on the assumption that some of the burden on family members providing home care can be alleviated. Rather than focusing on dementia as a disease, which cannot currently be cured, we look at those aspects of the situation which are manageable.

Our clinical experience has shown (and current research supports this) that caregivers experience stress either when they cannot manage the patient's behavior or when they feel isolated and unsupported. The application of the treatment strategies that follow are designed to improve the caregiver's ability to manage problems and increase his social support. Our intention is both to decrease stress so the caregiver will be in a position to maintain the dementia patient at home as long as possible and to help promote the caregiver's own health and well-being.

As discussed in Chapter 1, there are many psychological advantages of home care over nursing home placement. A familiar environment facilitates the patient's ability to function and thus lessens the need for controlling problem behavior with medication. Although nursing home placement may eventually be necessary, relocation should be considered in the context of all of the options available to the family. As we will see in this chapter, the burden on the family can often be maintained at tolerable levels, and nursing home placement can be delayed or even prevented altogether.

Intervention primarily focuses on the patient's family and not the patient. By the time a patient has been diagnosed, many families have already discovered the patient has a limited capacity for change. But some families may still be seeking a cure. Some caregivers may be reluctant to admit they need help with the patient; they want the patient to change. Often they will become involved in the treatment process when they understand that is the best way to help the patient.

In some instances, counseling might also be offered to the patient. It is helpful if the patient has an awareness of the problems, or is depressed. Even though the patient may not remember details of counseling sessions, clinical experience shows that these sessions seem to have a beneficial effect on mood. In the majority of cases, however, the primary focus of intervention is upon the family.

## THE STRESS-MANAGEMENT MODEL

In our work with caregivers, we have often improvised our techniques, drawing from general clinical skills and applying them to the specific problems of dementia patients and their families. As we became more experienced and got feedback from caregivers, some patterns in our approach have emerged. For the sake of clarity, we will break the treatment into its components. It is useful to think of both the content and process of what is being done, and to keep the intended outcome of the treatment in mind. These components will be called information (content) and problem solving (process). The purpose of the treatment will be to manage problem behavior and increase social support (see Figure 5.1). After describing the development and application of our method, we will illustrate in succeeding chapters how it is applied in three different modalities: 1. individual counseling, 2. family meetings, and 3. support groups.

**FIGURE 5.1.**
The Stress-Management Model for Families of Dementia Patients

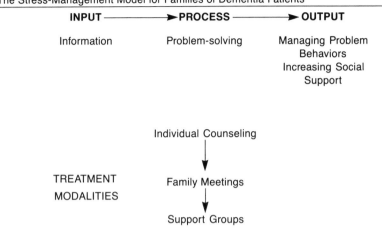

For our method, the information about dementia can be likened to data being entered into a system. When caregivers understand the patient's condition, they can learn to use a problem-solving process to solve *their* problems. If successful, problem behavior is managed more effectively and social support increased. This model is similar to other stress-management programs but differs in that the amount of information that must be considered tends to be greater because of the complexity of dementia. The focus of the treatment is on identifying the immediate causes of stress in the caregiver's situation and developing an intervention to alleviate the stress. In some cases, a caregiver can solve immediate problems but does not understand the disease. The intervention is then focused on providing information. In other situations the caregiver has plenty of information but is ineffective in dealing with day-to-day realities of the disease. We then focus on teaching the caregiver the process of problem solving. Ultimately, outcomes of managing problem behavior and increasing support to the caregiver can be either easy or difficult to achieve, depending on the patient's condition and the potentially available resources.

We use the stress management model in three treatment settings. Initially, we simply provided individual counseling for the primary caregiver on how to understand and manage dementia-related problems. Family meetings grew out of observations on the critical importance of social support to the primary caregiver and the impact that the dementia had on the family system as a whole. The patient's disabilities upset existing patterns of interaction and support among family members, and family meetings were established to restore balance to the system. We began holding support groups because of suggestions made by caregivers themselves that it was helpful to share experiences with other people in similar circumstances. Our first support groups developed as the result of a research study which brought caregivers together to show them how to teach the patient memory skills. While interaction among caregivers was not a goal of the study, it proved to be the most valuable part (Zarit, Zarit & Reever, 1982). Our use of groups parallelled developments in other parts of the country. Self-help groups often have sprung up in response to the lack of information and resources available to family members. The groups offer opportunities to pool information and to share some of the common problems and frustrations of being a caregiver as well as to support the caregivers themselves.

The usual pattern of treatment is to begin with individual counseling with the primary caregiver. After several sessions, the practitioner will try to arrange a family meeting. Generally, this is followed by the inclusion of the caregiver in a support group. (The order and time spent in each form of treatment can vary). Some caregivers may receive only a few sessions of individual counseling, followed by a family meeting. Others may need the intensive attention of individual counseling for a longer time. Support groups and family meetings provide different kinds of assistance to the caregiver than is available in individual counseling, for example, to learn from others in the same situation, or to resolve differences in the family about how to care for the patient.

Some service providers may not be in the position to provide all the treatment modalities due to limited resources. Thus, the discussion of interventions that follows can be viewed as a guide rather than a complete prescription. The important thing is to understand the conceptual framework which stresses maximizing the independence of the dementia patient while minimizing family burden. That goal can be implemented in various ways, depending on what works best in a given service site. (The stress management model is described in this chapter. Each of the treatment modalities are discussed in succeeding chapter.)

## TREATMENT COMPONENTS

### Information

When family members come to a clinic, they will have varying degrees of information about dementia. Some may be quite knowledgeable; others will have scant or misleading information. They may, for example, think that memory loss is an inevitable result of old age or is caused by hardening of the arteries. It is essential to give people accurate information. There are a number of reasons to do this first. It establishes the practitioner's credibility as someone who understands the problem. It helps alleviate the sense of crisis brought on by the family's dread about aspects of the disease. Many of the problems families experience arise from not knowing what to do or how to respond to the changes in their relative. Giving them information puts these problems in a workable perspective. The following case illustrates what can happen.

Mr. K., whose wife was moderately impaired, believed that her memory loss was caused by not trying to remember. He thought that if he could get her to exercise her memory, it would improve. Throughout the day he would repeatedly quiz her about names of people they knew, where she had put things, or about general information from news stories. She had a great deal of trouble recalling verbal information, which caused him to push harder and both of them would get frustrated and angry with each other. By helping Mr. K. understand that there was a physiological basis to his wife's memory loss, the counselor then was able to suggest a different strategy. Instead of quizzing her constantly, Mr. K. was encouraged to provide reminders when she needed help. Mrs. K., in fact, wanted this help, and made suggestions about how he could give it to her. She reacted positively to these reminders and Mr. K. reported his own frustration had decreased.

We do not prefer to overload families with information. We begin by asking them what questions they have, and what they already know. They may also be provided with some information pamphlets that describe the dementias. One useful brochure is "Questions and Answers: Alzheimer's Disease" available through the National Institutes of Health (NIH Publication No. 81–1646). Many caregivers find the information in the book, *The 36-Hour Day* (Mace & Rabins, 1982), to be helpful. Other books oriented to families have been written by Reisberg (1983), and Heston and White (1983). Books and brochures, however, *are not a substitute* for discussing information with the family.

The questions that families have can be divided into those related to the disease and those about the behavior problems it causes. In questions concerning the disease, the service provider can use the information presented in previous chapters to answer these questions. It should be noted that accurate information sometimes involves saying: "We do not know the answer, but these are the possibilities that have been considered." This approach is better than giving a definite answer that may be incorrect. For instance, instead of stating that acetylcholine deficits cause memory loss in Alzheimer's disease, it is better to say that is one of the hypotheses being investigated. If a family member asks a question for which the practitioner has no answer, it is better to admit that and try to find the information.

Questions about cures must be handled delicately, providing the family with accurate information without destroying all hope. While it is true that no treatment has been found that either arrests, reverses, or cures these diseases, some treatments can have a placebo effect. Studies using drugs on dementia patients often report no change on clinical scores due to the drug, although the family might report improvement. Since memory performance is unchanged, it is likely that positive expectations of family members leads to improved behavior, at least for the period of time studied. Thus, if a family wants to participate in a drug research study or try something relatively benign like vitamins or lecithin to help the affected member of the family, it may be worthwhile to encourage them. Trying a treatment sometimes gives families the feeling they are doing something for the patient. As long as they view a particular treatment as an experiment, and do not have overly high expectations, it can have a beneficial effect on them, and maybe even the patient.

Two difficult questions families often ask are: 1. can the disease be inherited? and 2. what is the course of the disease? There is considerable speculation about a genetic component to Alzheimer's disease, especially in cases of early onset (see Chapter 2). Research into genetic links has indicated that generally the risk that family members will inherit the disease appears to be small. Risk of inheritance is stronger if onset of the disease is before age 60, but inheritance is not suspected in late onset cases.

When families ask if the patient's condition will worsen, they are raising one of the most disturbing issues that must be faced. They do not know how long the problem will go on, or what to expect next. We recommend replying that no one can chart the course of an individual patient but there is usually a gradual decline in the patient. It is important to convey that the family should take each day at a time, dealing with the problems that arise. Descriptions of the worst possible case will only scare the family, and distract them from working on manageable aspects of their situation. At the same time, it is important to empathize with their concern regarding the uncertain course of the disease.

The other dimension of information to be conveyed to families is why patients behave the way they do. Explanations offered by the practitioner should try to reframe problem behavior, to help family members understand what the world must seem like to a person with impaired memory. A key component of these explanations should be to explore the patient's perspective. Table 5.1 presents several examples of common problems, how families often view them, and how the problems can be reinterpreted to them in the light of the effect of memory loss on the patient.

The impact of many behavioral problems can be mitigated by giving the family clear explanations of why they occur. Perhaps the problem most commonly complained about is that the patient engages in repetition, for example, asking the same question

**TABLE 5.1.**
Common Problems Reported by Families Viewed as the Result of Memory Loss

| Problem | Typical Interpretations | Interpretation When Viewed as Part of Memory Loss |
|---|---|---|
| Asking repetitive questions. | It is done to annoy me, attract attention. Patient could control it. | Patient cannot remember asking question or no longer has appropriate skills to get attention. |
| Patient is not aware of memory loss, denies it. | Patient should remember, why won't he face it? | Patient cannot remember he cannot remember. |
| Patient does not try to remember. | Patient is lazy, laziness causes the forgetting. | Some stimulation of memory may be helpful; patients may not be able to do this by themselves; if they become frustrated, it should be stopped. |
| Accusations (e.g. stealing) | Patient is crazy, just trying to hurt me. Patient does it to embarrass me. | This is one way of dealing with the insecurity caused by not being able to remember. |
| Lowered inhibitions. | Patient is trying to hurt me; patient should be able to behave himself; patient does it to embarrass me. | The brain damage often causes a loss of control. |
| Memory fluctuates from day to day. | Patient is not trying; patient is only remembering what he wants. | Some fluctuation in memory is normal. Fluctuation is not related to a lack of effort on the patient's part. It is important to take advantage of "good days." |

over and over again. Families sometimes believe the person does this on purpose to get attention. Pointing out that the patient may not remember the answer, or even having asked the question before, may help the family be more tolerant of the behavior.

Sometimes it is true that patients will ask repetitive questions to seek attention but they may no longer have other social skills for doing so. By understanding these limitations, the family can respond to the positive part of the behavior, the patient's request for involvement.

An issue which often comes up is whether or not the patient can control problem behavior. For instance, many families maintain that the patient should be aware that he asked the same question before. We point out that people with severe memory loss cannot consistently remember that they cannot remember or control problem behavior. Nevertheless, families may ask patients to set limits on themselves, such as not to walk too far from the house, or not to begin saying personal things to strangers. Of course, patients themselves may not have an awareness of their problems and may not be able to set limits on themselves. One of the more important and often difficult tasks for families is to set limits so that patients do not exceed their capabilities.

Memory will fluctuate from day-to-day in most patients; for some, it may be considerable. Families sometimes interpret these changes as a scheme by the patient to remember only what he wants to remember, or only when he wants to try. But patients may have little control over memory changes. Especially very early in the illness, family members who wish to deny the impairment may misinterpret a turn for the better as a sign that the patient does not have dementia. This leads to intensified disappointment when the patient becomes worse. (A positive aspect of fluctuating memory is the family can take advantage of good periods by interacting more with the patient.)

Families often wonder if something can be done to help the patient's memory function more effectively. Sometimes they believe that if they exercise the patient's memory, it will prevent it from getting worse, and may even improve it. Giving cues to help stimulate memory sometimes works, but if the patient is overwhelmed, families should be advised to discontinue the effort. In summary, memory exercises appear to have only a limited impact on memory functioning (Zarit, Zarit, & Reever, 1982). (Some practical memory aids will be discussed under problem solving.)

95

At some point, families will have to face the problem of when to deny some activities to the patient. In general, we advise families not to take over any activity unless the person cannot do it, or some danger is involved. By taking tasks away from patients, which they still may be capable of performing, such as dressing or cooking, they will forget how to do these things and will be unable to resume the activities at a later point.

Sometimes the patient's difficulties with an activity will be minor which can be helped with minimal assistance. For instance, one man reported that his wife could not get dressed. But when the counselor questioned him about the situation, it turned out she had too many outfits to choose from and mixed them all up. He found he could select an outfit for her and lay it out, and she would dress herself. As in this case, it is best to encourage families to offer minimal assistance or supervision, rather than to take over any activity. We have seen extreme situations in which families take over all functions from patients when the first signs of disability appear. This leaves the patients with nothing to do. Patients then become restless, nap during the day, and then do not sleep at night, and become a greater burden on the family.

Some activities such as driving or cooking involve risk or danger. What needs to be considered is not *should* dementia patients be allowed to continue to do these activities, but is this particular patient capable of doing so at that point in time. Some continue to drive or cook independently, but others need supervision. The service provider therefore must assess the degree of risk in each case. Is the patient burning food, leaving fires on, or driving unsafely? She must decide accordingly which activities must be supervised.

Families will also ask clinicians how much activity is beneficial for the patient. As was said above, we recommend allowing the patient to perform as many of the usual activities as possible. But this principle should not be carried to an extreme. That is, some families want to keep the patient at an extremely high level of activity, perhaps believing that increased activity will cure the disease. Forcing impaired persons to become overactive will only make them more anxious. This, in turn, can create frustrations for the family.

Also, when trying out new activities, the family should take into consideration that the patient may only be able to learn at a very slow rate and will likely have problems. Taking things slowly and allowing the person to adjust to the new situation will help alleviate their anxieties and frustrations. If the patient has problems in a new situation, such as the first visit to a day-care program, the family can be advised that adjustments can be expected to take time, and that at least a week's trial is needed before they make a decision about discontinuing the use of the center. In other words, there is a delicate balance between pushing the patient too much and not pushing enough.

Problems often arise when the brain damage causes a loss of inhibition. This can manifest itself in a variety of ways. Patients who were mild mannered may become angry. Formerly refined persons may begin using bad language, or dress provocatively, or start undressing themselves in inappropriate situations. Lowered sexual inhibitions can occur, especially in male patients. When families understand these changes are part of the disease, and not something being done deliberately to annoy or embarrass them, they can cope more effectively.

It is important for practitioners to explore fully each problem with the caregiver, showing how one can have a nonjudgmental response to the incidents. The caregiver's anger or embarrassment over the problems often negate logic, and sometimes solutions that are obvious to the counselor are not readily so to the caregiver.

One of the most disturbing behavior problems dementia patients may display involves paranoid accusations, especially that people are stealing objects or money. It is important to recognize that arguing or trying to rationalize with patients will not work. When families complain about this problem, describing how they have tried to reason, a counselor needs to point out that reasoning or arguing has not changed the patient's mind. The suspicion remains unshaken. The reason the accusations are made is that they cover up for the person's forgetting, where he actually had put the object, for instance. By arguing, the family is, in effect, trying to make the dementia patient confront his own memory loss, and most patients cannot do that. This is due to the fact that one impact of diffuse brain damage is to induce the afflicted person to shield himself from awareness of the disability (Zarit & Kahn, 1974; Weinstein & Kahn, 1955). Attempts to remind patients of what they have forgotten or to insist they acknowledge or confront their memory loss will only cause them to resist harder. A more successful solution is for the family to empathize with the patient's feelings of frustration or anger (e.g., over not finding a purse) but not to get into a rational discussion of the facts of whether or not it was stolen.

As these examples illustrate, providing information about why abnormal behavior occurs in those suffering from dementia is very important in working with families. Instead of viewing what patients say or do from normal standards or expectations, caregivers need to understand how brain damage has affected their relative. This is done by asking why they think a problem is occurring, how they think the memory loss has affected the patient, and by reframing problems in terms of memory loss. In other words, they learn to look at problems from the patient's perspective, as well as their own.

Understanding how memory loss has affected the patient's behavior must precede any interpretations on the part of the practitioner of caregivers' feelings or any attempts try to solve concrete problems. Without that understanding, caregivers will keep returning to the question, "Why is the patient doing that?" Or they will infer that they are doing something wrong, or the patient is just trying to annoy them. There is no therapeutic gain in getting caregivers to understand their own feelings when they are inaccurately interpreting the situations that give rise to those feelings.

The following case is an example of the importance of correct interpretation of the dementia patient's behavior.

The husband, who was the caregiver, had always managed the family finances, and was very exacting about it. One day his wife began asking about an old bank account, which no longer existed. He tried to explain rationally to her that they had used the money to make a different invest-ment, but she insisted that the money was still in the bank, and wanted to go there to take out money. When she ignored his explanation and kept asking the same question, he took it to mean she did not trust him to handle their finances, and became very upset. It is important to ac-knowledge his feelings (for example, "It must be hard not to feel trusted."), but also to provide him with an understanding of her behav-ior. In this instance his counselor explained that it is common for demen-tia patients to ask repetitive questions. She also suggested that an important issue like money may reflect his wife's insecurity, brought about by her inability to remember. After considering these explana-tions, the client responded to repetitive questions about their bank ac-count by reassuring his wife that their financial situation was sound, and no longer viewed her complaints as criticism of him. His reassurances appeared to reduce her anxieties, and she no longer asked him the ques-tions about the bank account.

## The Problem-Solving Process

Problem solving is a process for finding practical solutions to the immediate needs of the caregiver to control problem behaviors or to obtain more social support. It involves developing an alliance with caregivers in working out effective strategies for managing day-to-day problems. The relation between providing informa-tion and problem solving is complex. Understanding why prob-lem behavior occurs opens the possibility for problem solving. But in explaining to caregivers that the patient's problems are due to brain damage, there is a risk that the family will conclude that there is nothing they can do to improve the situation. Caregivers need to learn there are positive steps they can take, but they first have to understand that the normal rules of behavior do not apply.

The problem-solving process consists of a series of steps that lead to the development of strategies for controlling problem behavior or increasing social support (see Figure 5.2). Because the practitioner is teaching a process, the goal for the caregiver is to learn to apply the process from one problem to another, rather than becoming dependent on the practitioner for a solution to every different situation. The caregiver's progress may be im-peded by his or her emotional attachment to the dementia pa-

**FIGURE 5.2.**

The Problem-Solving Process
___

1. Identify the Problem
   a. antecedents
   b. consequences

2. Generate Alternative Solutions
   (no censoring)

3. Select a Solution: Pros and Cons

4. Cognitive Rehearsal

5. Carry Out the Plan

6. Evaluate Outcome

tient, and this must be responded to as well. The steps in problem solving are described below.

**Identify the Problem.** The first step in problem solving is to identify the most pressing problems. The practitioner should identify specific problems and when and how often they occur. One effective way of obtaining this information is by having caregivers keep a daily record or log. A sample of a daily record of the occurrence of problem behavior and the caregivers reaction is shown in Figure 5.3. The caregiver can be instructed to use this form in several ways. The first column is used to note the occurrence of a specific behavior (such as, asking repetitive questions). The second column helps to identify the caregiver's reactions to each incident; does he or she often get upset or feel stressed? This record is useful for identifying the specific behaviors which are most disturbing or difficult to manage. These behaviors can then be targeted for intervention. Also, when caregivers try out new strategies, they can note the results in the third column. Did the strategy work or not? There is also a place at the bottom of the form where the caregiver can note in general how stressful the day was.

One function of the assessment is to determine how often a problem occurs. The success of any interventions then can be

**FIGURE 5.3.**
Caregivers' Daily Record for Problem Solving

**Day:**

| Time of Day | Problem | Reaction | Outcome |
|---|---|---|---|
| Morning: | | | |
| Afternoon: | | | |
| Evening: | | | |
| Night: | | | |

Average Daily Stress:

| 1 | 2 | 3 | 4 | 5 | 6 | 7 | 8 | 9 | 10 |
|---|---|---|---|---|---|---|---|---|---|
| Not Stressful | | | | Moderately Stressful | | | | | Extremely Stressful |

assessed by changes in the frequency of the occurrences. The caregiver's ratings of stress can also be used as an indicator if the problem solving has been effective.

The assessment also provides information about what interventions might work by providing comparisons of what happened right before a problem arose, that is, its antecedents, and what happened right after some action was taken, or its consequences. When the daily records indicate that the problem behaviors typically follow certain antecedent events or always result in similar consequences, a possible way to avoid the behavior is to change something in that sequence. People who try to quit smoking must break the habit of smoking in a particular situation or during some activity, such as drinking a cup of coffee or after a meal. Similarly, the behavior of dementia patients often has a relation to certain events. With repetitive questions, for example, they may occur at times when the patient has been inactive (the antecedent), or may result in getting a lot of attention for the behavior (the consequence). Identifying these or other antecedents and consequences can assist in planning interventions to control problem behavior.

When caregivers use the daily record to track the patient's behavior, many common problems, such as not sleeping at night, are often found to be related to specific antecedents or consequences. Wakefulness at night is often viewed as part of the disease. Laboratory studies have found that dementia patients experience changes in the sleep cycle, including less time in deep (Stage 4) sleep and fewer hours asleep (Prinz, et al., 1982). But behavioral tracking sometimes reveals there are other causes as well. The patient may be inactive or napping in the daytime, and thus is restless in the evening. Daily records will help uncover the relation of specific behaviors with environmental cues which can be changed.

**Generate Alternative Solutions.** The next step in problem solving is to think of as many solutions as possible. Examining the daily records can yield obvious solutions. Clearly, when sleeping during the day contributes to problems at night, one solution would be to keep the patient awake during the day. If the cause of the insomnia is low activity, the patient should be given more things to do to tire him out.

Sometimes caregivers will find that problems occur only at certain times of the day and they can anticipate the problem and head it off. One caregiver, for example, observed that her husband became restless at 5 P.M. every day, but he calmed down after dinner. She simply moved the evening meal from 6 P.M. to 5 P.M. and found he was much less agitated.

Solutions, however, do not have to come directly from observations. A practical assessment of what might control problem behavior can suggest several alternatives. When the caregiver is thinking about alternatives, it is important not to prejudge the solutions. Rather, the caregiver should be encouraged to be as uninhibited as possible in proposing possible solutions.

**Choosing a Solution: Pros and Cons.** When the counselor and the caregiver feel alternatives have been listed, they can explore the advantages or disadvantages each might provide. It is often useful to write down pros and cons in two columns on a piece of paper (see Beck, et al., 1979). By setting out the benefits so clearly, the choice is often made easier. Generally, the caregiver should be encouraged to decide which solution will be best and the counselor should serve as the advisor.

**Cognitive Rehearsal.** When the caregiver chooses a possible solution to deal with a problem, the counselor should encourage the caregiver to carry out the steps mentally. This process is called cognitive rehearsal (Beck, et al., 1979) and allows the caregiver to anticipate problems he might encounter as he tries to overcome them. As an example, if the patient is slow in dressing, making others late as a result, one possible solution is for the caregiver to allow more time for dressing. Cognitive rehearsal involves encouraging the caregiver to rehearse this step mentally, for instance, by asking, "Is there anything that will keep you from allowing more time for dressing?" The caregiver, then, may anticipate possible obstacles, such as, "I will think to myself it will not happen this time, and so I won't take the extra time." The counselor can work with the caregiver to develop a strategy to anticipate talking himself out of leaving extra time, for example, by reminding himself that the problem will not go away on its own. As obstacles are identified, the caregiver and counselor can alter the plan. The goal is to develop a plan that the caregiver is willing and able to implement.

**Carry Out the Plan and Evaluate Outcome.** The final steps are to carry out the plan and evaluate the outcome. If the problem is now occuring less frequently, then the plan is having a positive effect. More perfection of the solution might reduce the incidence of the problem even more. If there is no change, however, then the solution is not working and another strategy is needed. Continued review of daily records will be useful for generating new solutions.

The problem-solving process can be illustrated with the example presented earlier in the chapter where the wife questioned her husband's handling of finances. The steps in problem solving were:

1. *Identify the problem.* The wife began asking about an old bank account, insisting that it still existed. She ignored her husband's explanations, and he believed she did not trust him to handle the money. The result was his feeling distressed. The frequency of these discussions was also recorded.
1a. *Antecedents.* His wife asking him for money.
1b. *Consequences.* Arguing with his wife and becoming upset.
2. *Generate Alternative Solutions.* The solutions which were discussed were:
   1. Continue to argue with her.
   2. Show her the cancelled passbook.
   3. Ignore her questions.
   4. Understand her inability to remember. View her questions as an indication of insecurity—this is the role of providing information. Then, with this understanding of the problem, reassure her when she asks that their finances are adequate.
3. *Select a Solution: Pros and Cons.* The first solution has led to the stress in the first place. Because the husband no longer had the passbook, Number 2 was impossible. He decided Number 3 would be more stressful than what he already was doing, so Number 4 was his choice.
4. *Cognitive Rehearsal.* After the caregiver selected the fourth choice, the counselor role played his wife, asking him questions about the account, so he could imagine himself responding differently in the situation. This is important because he may be arguing reflexively, and it may take some practice to break the cycle.
5. *Carry Out the Plan.* The caregiver tried reassuring her.
6. *Evaluate Outcome.* His reassurance calmed her down, and reduced his feelings of distress.

It should be emphasized that problem solving is a process of trial and error—there are no simple solutions. Solutions come partly from observations of antecedents and consequences and partly from the ability and preferences of caregivers. A solution which works for one caregiver to solve a particular problem may not work for another caregiver coping with the same problem.

Some caregivers readily accept problem solving. They are already doing it, or have done it before in other areas of their life. Some, however, feel too overwhelmed to try. They are angry at the patient, or they see it as the patient's problem, and reason the patient should change himself. For others, making a change means recognizing that this is a disease with problems that will not just go away. The reluctance to face this fact is understandable, given the terrible implication of the patient's having dementia. It is important to work carefully with these caregivers to encourage them to try problem solving, while conveying an understanding of their reluctance. In cases where the caregiver is just coming to understand the nature and implications of the disease, it is wise to proceed slowly, pacing the intervention to the caregiver's ability to accept it. You can encourage the caregiver to begin developing strategies by offering them as hypotheses or hunches. You can also offer illustrations as to how certain strategies worked for other people. The caretakers may simply need to hear that you are trying to do something for the patient.

The problem-solving process can be applied to any dementia-related difficulties. For instance, attempts to improve memory through the use of aids such as notes and reminders, can be made on an experimental basis. The caregiver can observe to what extent the patient forgets and when it happens. The caregiver can then introduce a memory aid when something is forgotten and then see if it makes a difference. The aid should be as simple as possible, and require only one or two instructions or pieces of information. When introducing a new memory aid, such as a blackboard to write important messages on, it is important to include repetitions as part of the plan so the dementia patient has a chance to learn to use it. If the patient can learn to use the aid or reminder, something important has been achieved. If it does not work, the caregiver has not lost anything, and in fact now possesses more information about the problem that will help in planning another form of intervention.

One key in planning memory aids and other means of intervening is to build on the dementia patient's old habits. The most successful use of memory aids we have observed was by a man who kept a daily diary to remind himself if he had eaten or done household chores. The use of a diary was quite familiar to him, since he had always used one extensively in his work as a writer. Patients who have used diaries, notebooks, notes, appointment books, or calendars in the past can be encouraged to use them, perhaps with some assistance from the caregiver. This will only be effective if the dementia patient had an efficient system. One 80-year-old retired doctor kept all of his notes and reminders on small slips of paper that he put in his shirt pocket. This system finally failed because he could no longer remember to put them in his pocket, but he was able to change to using a pocket-sized notebook.

A strategy which many caregivers find effective is to give the patient verbal or physical expressions of affection. Problems such as asking repetitive questions and restlessness are often diminished when the caregiver recognizes they are attempts to gain attention and responds with affection. The expression must be genuine, not forced, and to make sense in the context of the relationship between the patient and caregiver. Like other strategies, it will not work for some patients and in certain situations.

One woman was having trouble getting her husband to step off the curb to cross the street with the signal. He may have been confused by the many stimuli (traffic light, cars, people), or frightened by the swiftly moving traffic. She tried arguing with him and pulling him, but he would not budge. Finally, she took a deep breath and thought about it a minute. The next time the light changed in their favor she gently took his elbow and said, "Okay, honey, now it's time for us to cross." And he responded by letting her guide him.

This story was told in a support group and led other caregivers to speculate on different ways they might use affection to help them avoid conflict with their spouses or parents. Actually, caregivers seem more successful in using affection when the strategy is suggested by another caregiver (see Chapter 8).

When a solution for a problem which has been found to be effective in the past no longer works, the caregiver will typically assume that it is because the disease has progressed. Sometimes that is the case, but before accepting that conclusion, the counselor should inquire further into the reasons.

One man found that leaving a note for his wife telling her where he was prevented her from wandering out of the apartment when he was gone. At one point, however, she started wandering out again, and he assumed the disease had progressed. An inquiry by his counselor revealed that he had been leaving old notes around, as well as the current one. She did not know which to believe and wandered out to look for him. When he got rid of the old notes, and left only the current one, the problem ceased.

Of course, a new solution will often work, when an old method is no longer effective. A change in the dementia patient's response to any effort does not mean it is necessary to abandon problem solving, but may require a reexamination of the situation.

Record keeping sometimes reveals that the caregiver's reactions are the problem, not the patient's behavior. They overreact to the patient because of their frustration, or because minor incidents may symbolize the extent of their loss.

One woman who was caring for her husband tended to react very emotionally to even small problems. By keeping records, she recognized how her reaction contributed to the problem, and then was willing to try new responses. One night she found her husband staring off into space. When she asked what he was doing, he said, "Watching TV." She started to get upset as she had in the past, thinking "Oh, this poor man, how terrible." But she caught herself, and thought instead, "At least he's happy," and walked off to do something else.

In a similar example, a daughter reported that each time her mother asked, "When will you be coming home?" she felt angry and burdened. By keeping records of this sequence of events, she was able to identify that her mother's question signified she was trapped, and could not come and go as she pleased. Working with her counselor, she came up with alternative interpretations of her mother's questions: "She asks that question because she cannot remember." and "She is frightened by being alone." By reminding herself of these other interpretations of her mother's question, she no longer felt angry. She also took steps to make more free time for herself, so she would feel less trapped.

The result of record keeping clarified how the daughter response to her mother's memory loss. She could not initially identify why her mother's question made her so angry, and so daily records were used to make her more aware of her thoughts when she became upset. This use of daily records is similar to "thought records" in cognitive-behavioral treatments for depression and related problems (Beck, et al., 1979).

By keeping records of when problems occur, caregivers will sometimes discover that they happen less often or are not as severe as they thought.

One woman caring for her mother reported that her mother asked repeatedly when the caregiver's husband was coming home, and this made the daughter quite upset. When she began writing down when this occurred, she realized her mother did not ask her the question as frequently as she originally thought. Rather, the problem was that the question was irritating to her, because she interpreted it as a criticism of her marriage. As in the previous examples, record keeping helped her identify the real problem disturbing her.

Another outcome of record keeping is that caregivers realize they become upset by the accumulation of stress, and not by a particular problem. When that is the case, the solution is for the caregiver to learn how to anticipate when stress is building up and to develop plans to reduce it. Possible ways of managing stress have included asking someone to stay with the patient and going out, listening to music or doing a relaxation exercise.

**Applications of Problem Solving to Social Support.** The problem-solving process can be used to identify when the caregiver needs more support. In our experience, almost all caregivers could use more support than they are getting to cope with the continuous demands of caregiving, and the problem-solving process is useful in generating solutions.

Three types of social support are helpful: support received from a non-judgmental service provider, support from the caregiver's informal social network, and support from community agencies (see Figure 5.4).

The first source of support, the relationship between the caregiver and service provider, is an integral part of the intervention. A collaborative relationship, in which the caregiver feels listened to and understood, should be developed. The service provider brings technical understanding of dementia and the means for dealing with it. He helps caregivers decide what they want in a nonjudgmental and supportive atmosphere. Trust and confidentiality in this relationship are essential and make it more likely that the caregiver will try problem solving.

**FIGURE 5.4.**

Sources of Support

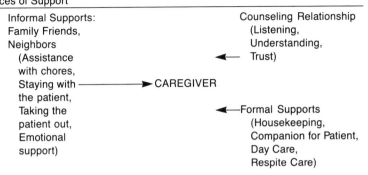

Informal social support is provided by family or friends and can be important in alleviating the feelings of burden of the primary caregiver. Caregivers are more likely to turn to relatives or friends for assistance than to social agencies. Help by friends and family can be provided in many ways, including staying with the patient, taking the patient out, housework, or transportation. The advantages of informal supports are that they are more flexible than those community agencies provide and do not cost anything. The problem-solving process can be used to determine what kind of support might be useful to the caregiver *and* that might be available from family members. Families and friends who are involved and supportive of the primary caregiver are a great asset. In cases where the family is uninvolved or conflicted, that can increase the stress of caregiving and is an appropriate place for family interventions (see Chapter 7).

Assistance from social agencies for housekeepers, companions to sit with the patient, day care, and respite care, can make the caregiver's task a lot easier. Identifying which services might help a caregiver can present difficulties. Services are not always available in every community. Moreover, the cost to families is often prohibitive, because of the lack of reimbursement from Medicare. In addition, many agencies are reluctant to serve dementia patients and some agencies which claim to serve the frail elderly actually have no training for managing them. They will drop the patient from the program at the first signs of problem behavior. A number of problems frequently cause community agencies to refuse service including wandering, verbal abuse, uncooperativeness, and inability to participate in activities with other older persons in the same program. A practitioner can work around these problems by providing training and consultation with service providers in existing centers and by working closely with the family and the staff of these agencies. The practitioner working with the dementia patient's family needs to learn the procedures of the various agencies in the community and to work with both the family and the agencies to optimize the amount of help that might be provided. Families should be told to present themselves to an agency in the best possible light. They need to ask for what a particular agency can provide, rather than laying out all their problems and letting the agency decide what to do. In our experience, the latter approach leads to being rejected for services. This approach can be illustrated with the following example.

A woman caring for her husband reported to us that he had wandered off from the house, but this had happened infrequently, and not in recent months. She was, however, still concerned about the possibility he might wander. When she considered the option of day care, she was advised not to focus on problems of wandering, but to evaluate what the program could offer her husband. Many day-care programs are reluctant to take anyone who has a history of wandering, and might automatically reject this application. But in this case it appeared the wandering had ceased and that the patient and family would benefit from day care. As it turned out, the man did well in the day-care program, and wandering was not a problem.

Even when services to assist the caregiver are potentially available, some will have great personal difficulty in asking for help or to accept it when it is offered. The caregiver may harbor beliefs about not seeking help, and the practitioner will have to encourage him to consider alternative ways of looking at the situation. Some caregivers think they should be able to do everything themselves. Other caregivers believe that their family or friends should know what help they need, and they should not have to ask. Still others think that asking for help is too much of an imposition on others, or that no one else could care for the dementia patient as well as they. In other cases, caregivers believe the patient would not accept the assistance.

As the service provider identifies potential sources of help, caregivers may express the beliefs which prevent them from accepting these suggestions. A clue that the caregiver has difficulty accepting help is when he responds to proposals by saying "Yes, but . . . . " As the reasons are identified, the service provider can, in a gentle, supportive way, ask questions that lead them to examine their beliefs about accepting help. For instance, when caregivers feel they have to do everything themselves, a counselor can ask what they think will happen if they do not take care of themselves by getting help, or if they think they will be able to continue providing care to the patient. Phrasing "accepting help" as something important they can do for the patient often makes a difference. Encouraging them to examine their beliefs by asking them questions is often more effective than directly confronting them (Beck, et al., 1979).

When a change in routine is introduced, such as hiring household help, the caregiver should be prepared for the patient's possible reactions. Dementia patients sometimes react strongly. Given time, we have found that most patients will adjust and even benefit from the changes in their routine. Caregivers can be prepared for the possibility of a negative initial reaction using cognitive rehearsal, so that they do not take it as a failure. When caregivers report they unsuccessfully tried services in the past, inquiring about the circumstances often reveals they did not give the dementia patient enough time to adjust. By explaining the importance of a long adjustment period, service providers can encourage the caregiver to try services again.

## SUMMARY

Interventions with families of dementia patients are based on the assumption that some of the burden they experience can be alleviated. A stress management model of intervention has been proposed, which is composed of three parts: 1. the input, providing information, 2. the process, problem solving, and

3. the output or goals, managing problem behaviors and increasing social support. Providing accurate information about the disease and answering the caregiver's questions about the effects on the patient's behavior and personality creates the foundation on which problem solving is based. Problem solving is a process for identifying possible ways of changing the patient's behavior, the caregiver's reactions to it, or gaining social support. This treatment is implemented by means of individual counseling, family meetings, and support groups, each of which are discussed in the next three chapters.

# CHAPTER 6

# INDIVIDUAL COUNSELING FOR THE CAREGIVER

When caregivers first seek help, the development of a counseling relationship will be very helpful in easing their burden and identifying positive steps they can take in caring for their relative. Individual counseling also sets the stage for more effective use of the other treatment modalities that include family meetings and support groups.

The goal of counseling is to identify ways of reducing the caregiver's stress by improving the ways they manage problem behavior and increasing their social support. Planning for a family meeting is also an important part of the individual counseling. These goals are implemented in the context of a therapeutic relationship in which the counselor is empathic and maintains a non-judgmental attitude.

There are several good reasons for beginning with one-on-one counseling for the primary caregiver. At the point at which they seek help, caregivers are often under a great deal of stress and need individual attention. They have a lot of questions and need some time to sort through the information they receive. The initial contact with an understanding and well-informed counselor who can empathize with the caregiver's experience is critical. This relationship sets the tone for the rest of the treatment process.

Some recommend alternatives such as providing case management, or placing the person in a support group. Our experience is that neither of these approaches is an adequate first step. Case management does not provide the opportunity for families to sort out what they want, to learn how to manage problems better themselves, or to receive the emotional support that they need. In addition, while the role of the case manager is to link clients to community service, these are not consistently available for dementia patients or their families. Support groups certainly can be beneficial (see Chapter 8), but they do not provide the intensive, individual attention that many families initially need.

## THE COUNSELING PROCESS

The counseling process should be problem oriented or concerned with the changes that the caregiver must face that have been caused by the disease. With this specific focus, counseling is brief. A typical case will consist of approximately seven counseling sessions, although some will take fewer and others may involve as many as 20 or 30 sessions. Often, followup is made by phone calls or an occasional counseling session, or the caregiver may join an on-going support group.

Counseling is focused on the specific problem of coping with the changes caused by the patient's dementia. In most cases, it does not involve in-depth, personal psychotherapy. The therapeutic approach is straightforward, and the caregiver will make rapid progress. The counseling relationship helps the caregiver use the information presented and mobilize effective problem-solving skills. Sometimes, however, the counseling process is more complicated because the caregiver is under a lot of stress or has difficulty learning how to problem-solve or ask for support. In these cases, several psychotherapy skills are very useful, including empathic listening (Rogers, 1951; Egan, 1975), behavioral problem solving (Lewinsohn, et al., 1977; Goldfried and Davison, 1976), cognitive therapy (Beck, Rush, Shaw, & Emery, 1979), relaxation training (Rimm & Masters, 1978), and systems and paradoxical approaches (Haley, 1976).

The first steps in developing a counseling relationship are to identify the goals of the caregiver, and to explain how counseling will help reach those goals. Goals are determined during the initial assessment. They reflect the most pressing problems presented by the caregiver although they may be general or specific. General goals include finding out more about the disease; seeing what options there are for community care; learning how to manage problems more effectively; or easing the strain of caregiving. Specific goals might be visiting a day-care program to see if the patient might attend; managing a *specific* behavior problem; or asking another family member for more help. The counselor and caregiver collaborate in identifying these goals.

The counselor will then explain how the counseling sessions will be used to attain the goals identified by the caregiver, for example, by using the problem solving process to generate new ideas for managing difficult behavior. It is important that caregivers understand that the sessions are centered on them, not on the patient. Some caregivers will expect that the practitioner will be able to do something directly to improve the patient's behavior. Sometimes this belief persists even after the counselor has explained that the purpose of the sessions are to help the caregiver.

In one case, counseling sessions with the primary caregiver were proceeding well. He was learning how to solve problems and to identify potential sources of relief for himself. In the sixth session, however, he told the counsel he had just realized the sessions were for him, not for his wife. The counselor was surprised by these comments. She had explained the purpose of the sessions to the caregiver during the initial assessment and again in their first counseling session. The caregiver went on to add that he had a lot more problems to work on, now that he understood the purpose of the sessions.

Although the outcome in this case was positive, the confusion over the results of the counseling shows a common problem. While the caregiver was discussing his wife's problems, it was his own behavior and reactions that were changing. At some point in counseling, this insight usually occurs to caregivers and may even be predictive of improved problem-solving skills. When caregivers have not yet reached a level of insight it is best to suggest the problem-solving strategies as an experiment to see the result. If a caregiver persists in seeking a cure and is unwilling to experiment with adapting to a current problem, it is wise to suggest that they continue their search for help elsewhere. If the caregiver understands that what is being offered is help in coping with current problems, he will be likely to return when new problems appear and at that time may be more amenable to suggestions.

To be successful with treatment process, treatment must be carried out in the context of an empathic and impartial relationship. If a caregiver does not feel understood by the counselor, then the treatment approach will not seem helpful. Caregivers are often frustrated because their usual ways of interacting with the patient no longer work. Furthermore, the recognition that the dementia patient is not going to regain normal functioning and will never again be the same person he was in the past saddens many caregivers. Before progress can be made, the service provider must acknowledge this sense of loss, so that the caregiver feels understood.

It is also important for the counselor not to be judgmental or to rush to present a lot of suggestions for what the client *ought* to do. In our experience, this is one of the most common mistakes counselors make. Caregivers may already feel guilty about not doing as well as they would like, or they may have been criticized by other family members. If the counselor is also judgmental, that can confirm the caregiver's sense of hopelessness that no one understands.

When, for example, a client describes getting upset frequently and yelling at the patient, one of the goals of counseling can be to reduce the stresses leading to that behavior. It would not be helpful however, for the counselor to say, "You should stop yelling. It only upsets you and makes the patient worse." Even a response like, "I understand why you yell, but it does not do you any good," misses the point. Those types of statements can make the caregiver feel bad and then do nothing to change the situation. Similarly, telling the caregiver he is in a particular stage of caregiving or has to get over his anger will not help. A more appropriate response might be: "The situation must really be frustrating for you. Many of the caregivers we work with report getting upset like that." This statement conveys understanding and acceptance, and lets the caregiver know his frustration is normal.

Counselors need to be able to make empathic statements that are spontaneous and genuine. This skill involves being able to identify the feelings expressed by the caregiver and then responding in a way that conveys understanding. In effect, the empathic statement involves looking at the situation from the client's perspective. Egan (1975) provides a useful guide for learning to make empathic statements.

The relationship between caregiver and counselor will also be strengthened by the counselor's providing information about dementia and the care of patients. Caregivers appreciate having their questions answered, and are often hungry for details. The counselor establishes herself as knowledgeable and trustworthy by providing accurate information or by seeking out information if she does not know the answer to a question.

As a therapeutic relationship develops, the practitioner can introduce the problem-solving process. In some cases, providing information about dementia helps caregivers use their own problem-solving skills. Many are already skillful problem solvers, and by providing them with information, the counselor points them in the right direction and they do the rest as this next example illustrates.

Ms. A., who was caring for her mother, described her job as a management consultant as helping solve other people's problems. When she discussed the difficulties she was experiencing with her mother, she could pinpoint the problems and identify antecedents. For instance, she noted that on some mornings she did not have the patience to give her mother the step-by-step verbal instructions that she had found necessary to help her get dressed. She further identified these were days when she had a lot to do. She had already planned an intervention, hiring someone to assist her on mornings when she had a lot of work, and wanted to know if that was a good idea. Clearly, this caregiver had good problem-solving skills.

If a caregiver is not good at problem solving, the counselor must work with him to figure out why and then develop a way to improve his skills. However, in some instances, caregivers are unable to apply these skills because they are under a lot of stress when they start counseling and feel too drained to make the effort these strategies require. If the caregiver is under a lot of stress and seems unable to make any changes, the counselor can concentrate on one key problem the patient poses, such as a difficult behavior, to which the caregiver can apply himself. Choosing an intervention which will result in an immediate result will encourage the caregiver to try other ideas. The solution has to be fairly simple, or the caregiver may not have the energy to implement it. The counselor's approach is important. It must be persuasive, but not nagging, understanding, and not rejecting. And when caregivers carry out the task, the positive results often make them amenable to more suggestions.

One woman was extremely stressed by the care of her husband, who was severely demented, and recently had become incontinent of bowel. She reported feeling overwhelmed by her problems and was reluctantly considering placing her husband in a nursing home. Initially, she was unable to use the problem-solving approach and could not even keep daily records of when the incontinence occurred. Gradually, however, her counselor was able to encourage her to keep daily records. After reviewing these records and information about his diet, the counselor proposed some modifications in his diet and a program of taking him to the bathroom on a regular schedule. This program worked immediately. The effect was to lower the stress on the caregiver and to make her more open to other uses of problem solving.

In some cases, caregivers will hold beliefs that prevent them from making changes. For example, they might think that since the disease cannot be cured, why bother to find better ways to cope? To overcome this attitude the counselor can ask them why they believe what they do, and then can present the task in a different way that overcomes their objection. If a caregiver doubts that an intervention will make a difference, one tactic is to ask her to try it as an experiment or to ask if she has anything to lose by trying. Beck and his associates (1979) describe procedures for questioning clients about beliefs that prevent them from coping more effectively with problems, and then explain how to challenge those beliefs in gentle but persuasive ways.

It is important for caregivers to keep track of how much stress they are experiencing when they begin to implement treatment procedures. The daily record form for problem solving (Figure 5.3) provides space for noting how stressful the day was for the caregiver. When a caregiver carries out an intervention, the stress score will reflect how successful it has been. Caregivers may somtimes report that an intervention has not worked despite the fact that their stress scores show improvement. The counselor can point out the lower stress and encourage the caregiver to continue the intervention. If a caregiver is disappointed that not all of the problems have been solved, the counselor can use the improved stress scores as evidence that the stress is less than before. For more suggestions on how to respond to clients who discount their gains in counseling, see Lewinsohn, et al. (1978) or Beck, et al. (1979).

Some caregivers tend to resist any direct suggestions, which necessitates modifying the problem-solving approach. In these cases, the client's resistance can annoy and irritate the counselor, who then cannot be empathic. When that happens, the counselor must step back from the problem-solving process and reestablish an empathic relationship. Once the client feels understood, the counselor then can reintroduce problem-solving methods using what Haley (1976) calls a "paradoxical directive." Since the client will reject any direct suggestions, the counselor phrases them so that rejecting them involves doing what the counselor wants. The use of paradoxical directives is illustrated in the following example:

Mr. T., whose wife had dementia, was very resistant to suggestions made by his counselor about alternative ways of handling problem situations. When the counselor became aware of his "Yes, but. . ." responses to her suggestions, she began responding empathically. After awhile, he told her he felt better, but she had not told him what to do. He wanted her to make a suggestion. Because he had rejected all her suggestions before, the counselor adopted a paradoxical approach. Instead of making a suggestion, she said, "There is one thing that might help, but I don't know if it would work for you." The client insisted on knowing what it was, and in contrast to previous assignments, which he had ignored, he carried this one out. For several sessions after that, he was able to make some progress in trying alternatives for managing his wife's behavior, and he developed a very positive relationship with the counselor.

While this client was able to respond to direct suggestions after that point, he reached another impasse that was resolved using the strategy of "covert" or "cognitive rehearsal" (Goldfried & Davison, 1976).

Although he continued to make progress, Mr. T. was unable to control his angry outbursts toward his wife. He said that because her condition fluctuated, every time she had a good day, he expected that to continue. When she functioned poorly again, he would lash out at her for not being able to do things. The counselor suggested that he remind himself that her condition fluctuated, but he was not able to do that. Finally, the counselor noted the similarity between his working out at a gym and his attempts to retrain his own thoughts about his wife's condition. Just as he had been unable to jump into the pool and swim two miles when he started working out, he could not expect to change his reactions to his wife without training. At that point, he accepted the idea of carrying cue cards, which he read twice a day, with statements such as: "My wife's ability to do tasks around the house fluctuates." and "Just because she has a good day doesn't mean that she has no problems." Eventually he was able to cue himself and remain calm in situations that had provoked his anger.

This case illustrates how several therapy techniques can be used to help caregivers overcome problems that prevent them from making changes that will improve their situation. The case study also uses multiple therapy; different techniques are used as the needs of the caregiver change and new problems are encountered.

One final purpose of individual counseling is to encourage the caregiver's independence. The service provider should emphasize teaching a process that can be applied to the caregiver's problems, rather than giving answers. Setting reasonable time limits for counseling often helps caregivers work toward goals, and not become dependent on the counselor.

## CASE EXAMPLE

### Case. Patti Jackson

**Introduction.** The following case illustrates the various issues that can arise in individual counseling with the caregiver of a dementia patient. In this case, counseling sessions were held regularly with the dementia patient's wife over a period of one year. The caregiver also attended several sessions of a support group. Although family issues were important, no formal family meeting was held. Over the period of counseling, the dementia patient experienced serious declines in functional abilities, which created problems in adjustment for his wife, Patti Jackson.

In the beginning counseling sessions, it became evident that the caregiver, Patti Jackson, had good problem-solving skills for managing her husband's behavior. She quickly learned to adapt the problem-solving approach to deal with his behaviors. She could use the suggestions made by her counselor. Rather than getting a sense of relief, however, she reported feeling upset and stuck. While she was now managing problems better, the counseling sessions also brought into clearer focus the fact that she was losing the relationship she had with her husband. At a critical point in the counseling, she was not even sure he recognized her or was benefiting from her caregiving. By coming to terms with this loss, she was able to become an effective problem solver again. This change came about gradually, developing from the context of the therapeutic relationship between the client and counselor, rather than from a didactic approach through which one might lecture the caregiver to accept her loss.

**Initial Interview.** Patti Jackson is a 56-year-old woman whose husband, Harold, who was 63, exhibited an abrupt change in behavior. He refused to go into work, or even to phone in an excuse. He was taken to see a general practitioner who reported finding nothing wrong, but felt he might be depressed. He was then taken to a private psychiatrist who prescribed Sinequan (doxepin), an antidepressant. Later, he was taken for a neurological workup which revealed no evidence of a tumor, stroke, or cardiovascular insufficiency which might have caused his abrupt behavior change. He was thus diagnosed with "early senility." (This type of vague diagnosis is, unfortunately, all-too-common, and leaves the family with little information or understanding of how they might proceed in the care of the patient.)

Dissatisfied with the information she had received from the hospital at which Harold had been evaluated, Patti brought her husband to our program for an evaluation. At the time of the initial interview, Harold was still able to dress and care for himself, although he had become quite irritable. He expressed resentment towards Patti for taking him to the doctors. But Patti herself felt the need for a better understanding of his problems, and how she might cope with them.

While Harold's family was aware of his condition, Patti was the only one who took care of him. As for other caregivers, this had been stressful to her. She had frequent telephone contact with the other family members, but did not receive their help in caring for him. Patti also had two daughters away at college, who knew about their father's condition. She felt it important to protect them from seeing Harold in his present state, and thus did not turn to them for any help.

**Initial Sessions.** Initially, counseling consisted of educating Patti about the disease her husband had and dealing with some problems. Harold was staying alone in the house during the day, while Patti was at work. At noon, he would go out to get lunch at a nearby senior center. While there seemed to be no risk at this time of his getting lost, Patti occasionally came home in the middle of the day to find he had left the door unlocked. Patti and the counselor came up with a plan to leave a sign on the door as a reminder, and to find out if that would make a difference. Patti came back and reported the plan had worked.

Another problem dealt with in the early sessions was the fact that Patti became irritated with Harold when he forgot to do chores around the house. When she reminded him he had forgotten to do something, he got upset with her, saying things like "You are trying to make me a patient." The counselor pointed out to her that Harold did not like to be reminded he had a memory problem, which is a common reaction of dementia patients. As an alternative, Patti decided she would just ask him to do the chore again, as if she had not asked before. This plan worked better for her; he no longer got upset about being asked to do the chores.

Patti also reported to her counselor that the physician had mainly described the problem as "getting older." With her counselor, Patti made a list of questions to ask the doctor, and she was able to get specific information, including the diagnosis that Harold was probably suffering Alzheimer's disease.

**Some Turning Points.** The early sessions increased Patti's ability to respond to day-to-day problems, and she felt better about her handling of the situation with each success. But Harold's condition continued to worsen, and new problems began to occur. Up to this point, Patti had viewed the changes in his behavior as part of the long-standing pattern of interactions between them, rather than as caused by the disease. Throughout their marriage, Harold had been secretive and had intentionally kept things from her. She viewed his recent changes in behavior as intentional, especially his forgetting, and believed that he was not revealing his motives to her. She responded as she had done in the past before the onset of the disease by trying to reason with him. Her efforts to help him remember or to get at his motives for forgetting only resulted in upsetting both of them.

Patti's difficulties in dealing with her husband came to a head when he no longer recognized her, and began insisting he was in a hospital, and she was the head nurse. She reported this behavior in counseling sessions, and her counselor helped her consider why Harold's refusal to recognize her was upsetting and how she could respond differently. While acknowledging Patti's frustrations, her counselor pointed out that trying to rationalize with him and reorient him to reality had not worked. As an alternative, they discussed asking Harold where he really thought he was, and who he thought she was. This was very difficult for her because she feared that he would confirm that he no longer knew who she was. She decided to take the risk, however, and when she went home that night she asked him where he thought he was, and more importantly who he thought she was. She was shocked by the fact that he really believed that he was in a hospital and that she was the head matron of the wing he was on. She then asked him if he was married, and when he said "Yes," she asked him what his wife was like. He proceeded to describe her as a beautiful, kind, and generous lady.

In retrospect, the incident described above represented the critical turning point in the therapy. Patti had made an attempt to communicate with her husband on a level of acceptance of his thoughts and his world. From this, she learned that he was responding to her efforts in caring for him by perceiving her as his nurse, and most importantly, that his behavior was not intended to hurt or upset her. She was the "wonderful matron who took care of his needs in the fine hospital he was in." There were other times when he thought she was his sister Ruth (whom he had always been close to), and at times he recognized her as his wife. Although he did not always recognize her, she came to understand that his misperceptions were ways he expressed positive feelings toward her for the care she was providing.

The changes in Patti's perceptions described above illustrate how information about the meaning of the dementia patient's behavior can have positive results for the caregiver. The meaning of her husband's failure to recognize her was too frightening for Patti to confront directly or all at once. Recognizing Patti's anguish, the counselor worked first to convey to her an understanding of the situation and then to clarify why this problem was so difficult for her. In that context of trust and empathy, Patti was able to understand her own reactions and take the chance that she did to understand her husband.

At this point, Patti was able to progress in dealing with day-to-day problems. The counselor once more began stressing the problem-solving approach to caring for her husband. This technique is best exemplified by the planning involved in an impending trip to Chicago for their daughter's college graduation. By this time, Patti was quite aware of the disruptive effects travel can have on a dementia patient. With her counselor's collaboration, she planned how to minimize those effects. First, she decided to stay in a hotel rather than with relatives. She felt it would be more likely that Harold would be upset by the numbers of people he would come in contact with if they stayed with relatives. Because she was concerned about the disorientation he would experience when he got up at night to go to the bathroom in a strange room, she called various hotels in search of one with a room that was arranged like their own bedroom. As he had always been fearful of buses, she planned for transportation via taxi cabs. The only situation she found impossible to solve was that of the commencement ceremony itself. She knew it would be crowded, and it would be inconvenient if her husband decided he had to go to the bathroom during the ceremony. She brought this problem to the session and worked through it with her counselor, discussing how she would handle the situation if it did occur. The trip worked out well, and he did not become upset at any point, although he was annoyed by the crowd at the graduation. He did not seem to know what was going on during the ceremony. Nevertheless, later that fall Patti overheard Harold telling a friend that he was so proud of his daughter and that he had been to her graduation. This example is remarkable because he did not seem aware of her graduation at the time. By treating him as though he was aware, Patti was able to provide him with a positive experience which he benefited from, despite his dementia.

Another instance of Harold's perceptiveness was noted in his reaction to his mother's death. His mother, 92, had taken ill, and Patti decided that she would tell him of it. His mother had always been the traditional matriarch of the family, and she felt it would be important to Harold to know of her impending death. He exhibited few signs of understanding and showed no emotion when she told him. His only comment was "Oh, Mama's sick . . . poor Mama . . ." The next morning he spent 15 minutes searching for his mother, something he had not done previously. His mother had died during the time he was searching for her. During his mother's funeral, Harold showed no understanding of the event. A few days later, however, Patti found him crying, saying "Mama's gone."

**Medications.** As with many dementia patients, Harold had been placed on a schedule of medications. He had originally been on a combination of Haldol and Mellaril, and then was given other drugs to control the side effects produced by the first two. Early in the counseling sessions, Patti had described his behavior as characterized by outbursts of anger and even violence at times. He also kept Patti awake at night. In order to find out if the medications were having an adverse effect, Patti was taught how to keep a record of his daily behavior, noting when problems occurred. She was therefore able to determine how often problem behavior occurred. As the medications were changed, she then could determine if the frequency of problems increased or decreased. The medications were gradually reduced, while at the same time Patti increased the amount of Harold's activity during the day. This combination of changing the dosage of the drugs and increasing activity reduced the outbursts and wakefulness at night. By the fourth month of counseling, she had reduced his drug intake to 2 mg of Haldol per day. She described his resulting behavior as strikingly more alert. He had become more talkative and was again recognizing Patti as his wife. Apparently, Harold had been exhibiting a toxic reaction to the medications he had been taking. Although emotional outbursts and changes in sleep pattern are often considered part of the dementing illness, this example illustrates how too much medication can also cause these problems.

**A Life of Her Own? Support Issues.** When she first came in for counseling, Patti was able to leave her husband alone at home during the day, while she went to work. After a few months, it became apparent that Harold could no longer find the senior center where he had lunch, and there were other times he wandered off from their home. As these changes developed, Patti had been gathering support services, including help with housework, and some supervision for Harold. She had been considering the option of retiring so that she could spend all of her time with her husband. Caregivers often give up all their other work, and social and leisure activities, and later report feeling resentful, or just simply exhausted from not having anything else in their lives. For that reason, Patti was encouraged to try to continue working, while using community resources to maintain

Harold at home. Guided by her counselor, she decided to explore the alternative of day-care services first, which turned out to be effective for almost a year. This allowed her to work, while having the reassurance that Harold was in a secure environment.

The issue of having a life of her own proved much more difficult for Patti. She had to get up and see that Harold got dressed and to the day-care center, go to work, pick up Harold, and then spend the evening tending to him. She could not arrange for some time for herself. One alternative discussed in the counseling sessions was to involve her daughters more. But Patti believed that it would be harmful or detrimental to them to get more involved in their father's care. Her counselor helped her develop alternative ways of viewing the situation, and eventually helped her to reconsider the situation by showing how the daughters might be benefitted by being involved in their father's care. This was achieved through a process of asking gentle, but probing questions to help Patti explore the assumptions she held about caring for her husband and the consequences of her actions. See Beck, et al. (1979) for a description of this kind of questioning. In this way, Patti grew to recognize the desirability of having her daughters care for Harold especially if she was no longer able to care for him. She also realized that it was very important for her daughters to give support to her. In addition, she recognized the emotional distance she created between herself and her daughters by not giving them the opportunity to care for Harold, which in turn contributed to her feelings of "being alone."

**The Role of Record Keeping.** The counselor attributed much of Patti's progress in therapy to her efforts and ability to keep daily records. She initially accepted the idea that the records would indicate if there was any pattern to his problems. As she continued recording Harold's behavior throughout counseling, she began to see patterns in it. If there was a change in his behavior, she was able to pinpoint an incident that precipitated that behavior, for example, a change in Harold's medication schedule. On one occasion, he abruptly became very agitated, talked incessantly, and exhibited outbursts which had ceased for quite some time. She could not find either medical causes, nor situational precursors to this change. In retrospect, she and her counselor linked this change to a time during which Patti was experiencing an increase in stress outside her relationship with Harold. He was in fact responding to her tension.

**Outcome.** Harold's behavior eventually began to deteriorate again, and Patti could no longer control the problems well. He became constantly restless and disruptive and had begun urinating in the heat ventilators and talking loudly in the middle of the night. The day-care program also could not manage him. At that point, Patti decided to place him in a nursing home. Patti was satisfied with this decision. She recognized that she had exhausted any and all alternatives that might help her in caring for her husband. She also knew that she had done everything possible for Harold, keeping him at home for as long as possible. She reported feeling no guilty thoughts, and felt a great reduction in stress.

In retrospect, the counseling process enabled Patti to provide the kind of help to Harold that she wanted him to get, without placing too much burden on herself. As his condition deteriorated, she reached out first to formal services, such as day care, and later to her daughters for the assistance that she needed. She believed she was fulfilling an important obligation to him. While he eventually was placed in a nursing home, it was done with Patti and her family knowing they had done their best.

## SUMMARY

This chapter has described individual counseling for caregivers of dementia patients. The stress-management model is introduced, first by providing information, and then teaching caregivers the problem-solving process for managing the patient's behavior and increasing their social support. This treatment approach is implemented in the context of a therapeutic relationship. It is especially important for the counselor to be empathic and to maintain an impartial attitude. While some caregivers respond quickly to these interventions, others have more difficulty with problem solving. Specific techniques can be used to overcome these difficulties and to help caregivers cope more effectively with the burdens that their relative's dementia has placed on them.

# CHAPTER 7

# FAMILY MEETINGS

The amount of the burden caregivers experience caring for a patient is related to the support they receive from family and friends. In many cases, individual counseling proceeds well for a while, but then no further progress can be made without involving the family. Family meetings can directly lower the stress of the caregiver and often result in impressive changes.

The family meeting usually takes place in one session. (Followup often is conducted just with the primary caregiver.) On rare occasions, we have held second family meetings but find that one session is usually sufficient. Positive steps can be taken after only one session, because the focus is on responding to the changes caused by the dementia, rather than on long-standing family conflicts or pathology. Our experience has been that most families can readily use information the counselors provide related to dementia and agree to give more support to the primary caregiver. In that respect, the family meeting follows a crisis intervention model of identifying existing sources of help rather than trying to create them. Only in instances of severe, long-standing family difficulties has the family meeting not been successful.

From a broader perspective, the family meeting addresses the tensions and imbalances in the family system created by the dementia patient's disabilities. The patient had a particular role in the family and carried out specific tasks. As the patient's impairments increase, there is more pressure on others to take over tasks; some important functions may not even be carried out.

This is especially the case with affective tasks, such as maintaining contact among family members or being a confidante. These functions are harder for families to identify than instrumental tasks such as managing the finances, but their absence produces similar or even greater strain on the system.

In planning a family meeting, one task for the practitioner is to figure out how the family system has been disturbed by the patient's illness. Families know something is wrong, but they place the problem upon the dementia patient. As long as they blame the victim (or in some cases, the primary caregiver) for not being adequate to the task, nothing changes. When the patient's problems can be viewed as part of the larger family system, and it can be understood that the family has undergone changes, then progress is possible. The family meeting is useful both for assessing changes in the family caused by the dementia and identifying ways of compensating that can bring the system back into balance. Families probably present more variety in their organization and operation than any other informal or formal social institution. The role the dementia patient played in a family and how the family system functioned will, of course, vary from one case to another.

While functions are sometimes divided along sex lines, with men carrying out instrumental tasks and women providing more of the affective dimensions, there is also considerable sharing of activities, or instances in which the wife handled more instrumental tasks while the husband was the emotional center of the family.

Moreover, the impact of a loss on the family will vary depending on how much they valued the activity or function that the patient previously carried out. For instance, having a clean, spotless home may be important to some families. If the patient was primarily responsible for housekeeping, then her inability to continue her role will have more impact than in families where housekeeping was not so highly valued. Similarly, some families stress elaborate family get-togethers. If the dementia patient was the organizer of those gatherings, then the cessation of the gatherings will place considerable strain on that family.

When caregivers bring up their feeling of losses, they often are referring to how they miss what the patient brought to the relationships in the family. Some valued the patient for various activities such as cooking or managing finances. Others miss the dementia patient's conversation, companionship, intellect, or sense of humor. These types of losses are difficult to replace, but at least can be recalled. If there are tasks that are necessary for the functioning of the household that are not being carried out, then it is important to work with the family to figure out who might take over.

The individuals who are available to take over tasks varies from family to family. When the primary caregiver is a spouse, that person often tries to take over most of the responsibilities, which creates special burdens. Husbands, for example, often are faced with learning how to perform household tasks they are unfamiliar with, and they may feel inadequate. They also might compare themselves with the way their wives ran the house. Wives may try to continue to run the household as they had before, even though they now have caregiving responsibilities. Children who take on the role of primary caregiver vary considerably in what they are willing and able to provide. One limitation on their caretaking is their responsibilities to their job and their own spouses and children. Another factor is proximity. If they live too far from their parent, there are fewer tasks with which they can assist. Their prior relationship with the patient and with the primary caregiver also affects what they are willing to provide. Generally, the more positive the relationship, the more children are willing to give.

The other dimension to consider is how the family functions as a whole. Important questions are: Who makes decisions? How are decisions made? What alliances are there between family members? What long-standing conflicts or feuds are there? What place in the family hierarchy did the patient and primary caregiver have? Interventions are made within the established framework of family interactions, rather than by trying to change family structure.

## PLANNING THE FAMILY MEETING

In preparing for the family meeting, the clinician needs to consider the timing of the meeting, the place it is held, who is invited, and how it is arranged. The timing of the meeting depends on the progress the primary caregiver makes in individual counseling. The critical factor is to identify the specific problems facing the caregiver, what support would be helpful, and the ability of the caregiver to ask for help. (There are numerous ways to provide support including weekend respite, someone to sit with the patient, assistance with shopping, or receiving more frequent calls from family members.) It is also helpful if the caregiver has gained insight into the means of problem solving. That is, rather than viewing the problems caused by the patient as insurmountable, the caregiver learns to think about ways of managing problem behaviors or the stress they create. Caregivers are usually ready for a family meeting after five or six counseling sessions, but some require fewer sessions and some need several more sessions.

The best place to hold family meetings is in the home of one of the family members. There are number of reasons that meetings in the home are preferable. The home meeting enhances the clinician's credibility with the family. The home is also a more comfortable and relaxed setting. When called into an office, relatives may become defensive about their role in caring for the patient, but they are more likely to feel in control of the situation in a familiar setting. It is preferable to hold home meetings in the evening or on weekends. Finally, families often plan a social event after the meeting, which enhances the positive atmosphere. [One risk to practitioners who regularly hold family meetings is overeating, since relatives usually provide homemade refreshments!]

People who are part of the social support system should be invited to the family meeting. Anyone the caregiver perceives as having an important role can be asked to come. Immediate family such as children or siblings are, of course, important, but others may have a role, including grandchildren, nieces and nephews, or cousins. Friends or neighbors who are identified as important supporting persons also should be invited.

A complicated issue is whether or not the patient should come to the family meeting. Some families do not want to talk behind the patient's back. Others feel they cannot talk freely with the patient present. There needs to be some consensus on this issue before the meeting. There is no clinical evidence that the presence or absence of the dementia patient affects the outcome.

People attending usually come just from local areas, but at times relatives from out of town also attend, especially if the meeting can be coordinated with their visit.

One large family meeting coincided with the patient's granddaughter's wedding. The primary caregiver was the patient's daughter, and it was particularly important for her sister, who lives overseas, to attend the meeting. Despite the great distance between them, the sisters had regular contact through letters and calls, and the sister living abroad was a major potential support for the sister who was caregiver. By holding the meeting around the time of the wedding, the sister who lives overseas could attend. Her presence at the meeting turned out to be critical. Her understanding of her mother's problems increased, and she became more aware of the pressures on her sister. She played a positive role in the meeting in rallying the support of other family members around her sister.

The meetings we have held have varied in size between two to twenty persons. When the number of people attending the meeting exceeds four, the interactions among family members can get very complicated, and so two counselors are recommended. One counselor should be the one with whom the primary caregiver has been working. This counselor plays a more active role in setting the agenda of the meeting. The other counselor plays a supportive role but may be especially useful by bringing a fresh viewpoint. While the first counselor is more closely allied with the primary caregiver, the second can think about family interactions from a systems perspective.

## THE STRUCTURE OF FAMILY MEETINGS

The goal of the family meeting is to implement the stress-management model, first by providing information so that everyone has a good understanding of the patient's condition, and second, to introduce the concept of problem solving. While some attention may be given to managing problem behavior, problem solving is often focused on how to increase support to the primary caregiver.

The counselors can start the meeting by stating that it is an opportunity for the family to get a better understanding of the situation and then encourage them to ask questions. Some family members may misunderstand the patient's problems or the caregiver's responsibilities. The counselor can provide accurate information.

One common problem is for persons not directly involved in day-to-day contact with the patient to view the patient as unchanged. They may fail to recognize there is a problem, or may not understand the disease as completely as the primary caregiver does. For instance, children sometimes expect a cure for the disease, but their parent realizes that there is none. Or children might want to take the patient to more doctors, while the parent wants to get the children to provide more help. By providing accurate information in response to the family's questions, the counselors increase everyone's understanding of the dementia. This helps the participants view the family system as having changed, and makes it possible to develop new patterns of interaction.

An important conflict in some families surrounds assigning blame to one person for causing the disease.

In a situation involving a husband caring for his wife, both of their daughters were convinced that their father's odd behavior (he was a lifelong agoraphobic) had caused their mother's deterioration. Information provided at a family meeting helped them understand that their mother's condition was due to a brain disease, and was not a mental illness brought about by their father's behavior. They were encouraged by this information, and were able to look at their father a little more positively. A key turning point came some months later when their father had to be hospitalized because of a medical emergency, and they assumed the daily care of their mother. After caring for her for one week, they understood how difficult it was for their father and gained new respect for him. Since that time, they visit more frequently and are no longer critical of him for the way he cares for her.

Although the major changes in this case took place several months after the family meeting, the meeting was the first step in rebuilding the relationship between father and daughters.

Once they understand the disease and its impact on the patient and the primary caregiver, the family is then encouraged to think of various ways to provide more support. The best approach is for the caregiver to identify some specific needs, such as having more time to one's self, being able to get out on occasions, or having overnight respite. The family can then be asked to meet this request. It is best not to expect that the family will propose a particular solution but to let solutions emerge that reflect what they are able to carry out, as well as their own values. When a family does not have good problem-solving skills, then the counselors can guide them to identify and clarify a problem and generate possible solutions. As family members come to understand the problem-solving approach, they can gradually take over running the meeting.

## THE PROCESS OF FAMILY MEETINGS

The solutions to problems caused by the dementia come out of using the family's own resources and problem-solving methods. While the counselors know something about the family's interactions before the meeting, their knowledge is limited since it has come largely from the primary caregiver. As the meeting unfolds, they need to observe the pattern of interactions in order to plan effective interventions.

There are a number of critical observations for the counselors to make about family interactions. Is the family getting off the subject as they discuss the problems caused by the dementia? Whose opinions are given more credence? What is the role that the dementia patient played in this family system? What is the caregiver's role in this system? Is the caregiver powerful or viewed as inadequate by other family members? Are there long-standing family conflicts or problems?

The success of interventions depends on figuring out how problems get solved in a particular family, and then supporting or augmenting that process. The focus of the family meetings should be on problems relating to the dementing illness. Some families may have long-standing conflicts, which potentially could erupt during the family meeting. Our experience is that families in conflict can usually cooperate on the issues surrounding the illness, without first resolving the problems of their relationship. The counselors, however, should be aware of any conflicts before starting the meeting and be prepared to redirect family members away from those issues and toward the caregiver's situation.

Often, as the meeting unfolds, a natural problem solver emerges; that is, someone in the family takes charge and begins to propose various ways to deal with the problem. This is the ideal pattern because it means the family will be better able to maintain the problem-solving process after the family meeting. If no one emerges as a problem solver, then the counselors can play a more active role in problem solving. After posing the problem, such as, the caregiver would like to get away for a few hours a week, the counselor can ask for suggestions or alternatives as to how this could be brought about. It is important not to pressure family members to volunteer to take over the task of providing care, but rather to allow possible solutions to emerge that indicate what each is willing and able to provide. Solutions can include having relatives do more to assist the primary caregiver, or identifying friends or neighbors who can assist, finding help at church or from other voluntary groups, or hiring someone to provide the help.

When relatives volunteer solutions, the counselors should watch for the person who will overcommit his or her services and may not be able to follow through. The counselors can tactfully intervene, ask if it is possible to carry out all those tasks, and then help generate a more realistic number of tasks.

The main criterion for solutions is that they work well within the family system. Do they use available resources as well as implementing the family's values? Some families will be more willing to volunteer time and resources; others will prefer purchasing services. In either case, it is important to work with the needs and the resources of the family.

Another task for the counselors is to create a supportive atmosphere within the family meeting, especially since social support is critical in reducing the primary caregiver's burden. When family members make supportive statements, the counselors can reinforce them. Nonsupportive statements can be redirected, or rephrased if they are latently supportive. For example, if a son complains about some aspect of how his mother has handled his father's dementia, the complaint can be stated as indicating concern for the caregiver (Haley 1976).

An important feature of family meetings is that everyone involved in the system can be brought together at the same time to clear up misunderstandings or to bring out into the open a hidden problem or conflict. In doing so, however, the counselors need to be careful not to take sides and to keep any disagreement or conflict within limits, so that compromises might be made. The following example illustrates how the face-to-face interaction in a family was used to resolve a potentially serious conflict between brothers.

Bob, whose mother had dementia, called the clinic for an appointment, and specifically requested a family meeting. On the phone he stated that he and his sister, Frances, had been supervising their mother's care, but their other brother, Ted, had not followed through on the tasks they asked him to do. Because the family had not been seen before in the clinic, we asked to meet with him and to evaluate his mother's condition before holding the family meeting. Before bringing the family together, we wanted to confirm that the mother did have dementia and to learn more about the family conflict. An evaluation of the mother revealed she did have symptoms of dementia, but the degree of cognitive impairment was relatively mild. In the interview with her, she stated she always felt closest to her son, Ted, the one who was not now involved in her care.

The family meeting was held the next day. Timing of the meeting was critical because this was the one weekend a month that Frances came into town to assist her mother, and it was important that she be present. The meeting opened by answering questions the three children had about their mother's condition and the suitability of the arrangements they had made to maintain her in her own apartment. They were concerned about the risk to her of getting lost or hurting herself while cooking, and these issues were discussed and resolved. Then Bob raised his complaint that Ted had not done his share. Rather than replying defensively, Ted agreed. He said he knew he had been letting his brother and sister down, but he had always been the closest to their mother, and it was too hard for him to visit her now that she was impaired. When Bob and Frances understood why he had not done his part, they were no longer angry, and the three of them worked out a new way of distributing responsibilities. Ted took on financial tasks that did not require him to visit, but he also said he thought he would now be able to go see his mother.

This session was typical of successful family meetings in that the outcome involved a better understanding of what each person could do. It also permitted them to come together as a family, sharing their strengths and limitations in an atmosphere of acceptance, rather than blame or guilt.

Another example of using family meetings to bring difficult problems into the open is when there are complicated questions about the patient's care. In the following example, the patient's dementia was caused by a potentially reversible condition, a blocked artery leading to the kidneys, but surgery to remove the blockage involved high risk. The family meeting was used to discuss the pros and cons of the surgery. Issues of support for the primary caregiver also emerged.

Mrs. Crawford, aged 77, was brought to the intake by her daughter, Martha. Martha reported that Mrs. Crawford had been having mild memory problems for about eight months. Four months before the appointment, there was an acute flareup which was probably due to the many medications she was taking at that time. She was hospitalized and the medication regimen adjusted. Upon her release from the hospital, she was able to return home.

Mrs. Crawford lived alone in a house, which was next door to her daughter. Martha was concerned because her mother had recently started having more trouble remembering to take her medication. She was also concerned about her safety because Mrs. Crawford took short walks in the neighborhood and had been robbed once. Martha had been able to watch over Mrs. Crawford, but her youngest child had just gone off to college and she was planning to go to work. She was worried that without her supervision, Mrs. Crawford would not be able to stay in her own house.

A neurological examination had never been done, so one was recommended. The neurologist noted the relatively brief history of cognitive symptoms and evaluated the medications Mrs. Crawford was currently taking. After completing his examination and getting the results of lab tests, he concluded that Mrs. Crawford's cognitive difficulties were probably caused by a blocked artery to her kidney. While this problem can be corrected by surgery, the doctor noted her frail physical condition and said he felt she was a high risk for surgery. He also noted that her cognitive functioning was partly related to the medications she was taking, which were necessary to control the renal problem.

After completing the workup, a family meeting was scheduled to discuss the results and Martha's need for support. Mrs. Crawford attended the meeting. The initial discussion focused on the doctor's findings. The family and Mrs. Crawford all agreed to go along with the doctor's recommendations not to have surgery. The focus of the discussion then shifted to ways of compensating for Mrs. Crawford's impairment. The major concern was if she was safe living alone. Martha presented her preference to go back to work. Another of Mrs. Crawford's children, who lived nearby, agreed to visit Mrs. Crawford at noon to make sure she was all right. Mrs. Crawford also agreed to go out for walks with her grandchildren who would come by after school, rather than going out alone.

This family was able to consider the difficult question of whether their mother should undergo high-risk surgery in the family meeting. They reached the consensus that the potential gains, which included reversal of her mild cognitive deficit, was outweighed by the risks. The responsibility for the decision was shared among them, rather than falling on one person. Followup indicated that Mrs. Crawford's condition had stabilized, and she was still able to live independently six months later. The family meeting also provided the forum for Martha to discuss her plans for going back to work and to identify the specific problems that created for Mrs. Crawford's care. Because her impairments were mild, only minimal supervision was needed and other family members readily volunteered to provide it.

## FOLLOWUP

Followup of family meetings is important to insure that suggestions have been carried out. Typically, the followup is handled by holding a counseling session with the primary caregiver, although other family members may attend. (In some cases, if the caregiver or relatives live at a distance, followup is conducted by telephone.) The followup assessment may indicate that some adjustments need to be made in the plan that had been worked out at the family meeting. Adjustments can include changing some assigned tasks or responsibilities, changing the schedule for responsibilities, or decreasing the assigned tasks.

If the plan that had been agreed upon is not being carried out at all, then a second meeting could be held. Possible issues to explore at that meeting are to determine if people overcommitted themselves at the first meeting, and what has interfered with carrying out the tasks. As in the first meeting, the counselors should maintain a positive and impartial tone. Rather than making people feel guilty for not having done their tasks, the counselors can reframe the result as an experiment which has taught them that these arrangements do not work. They can reinforce the family's good intentions and try to come up with a realistic plan.

After the followup visit, the counselor and primary caregiver usually will terminate regular appointments, although the counselor can remain a resource for the caregiver or other family members when they have questions or if new problems come up. The caregiver may also want to call the counselor periodically to provide progress reports. Families may want to hold periodic meetings among themselves and should be encouraged to do so. After completing the family meeting, the primary caregiver, and sometimes other family members as well, might want to join a support group, which can be useful in maintaining gains made in individual and family counseling, as well as adding some new therapeutic dimensions.

## CASE EXAMPLE

### Case. Mrs. Thompson

The following case is an example of a family meeting with some relatives who held long-standing grievances. The meeting was successful because the focus was kept on the immediate issues of the mother's dementia. Another feature of this meeting was the leaders did not have a counseling relationship with the primary caregiver. Because of the distance he lived from the clinic (over 80 miles each way), he was not willing to come for counseling and was also skeptical about his need for it. The person who sought help was his step-daughter, who was concerned that he was not managing the problem well. She arranged the family meeting.

**Initial Assessment.** The initial assessment interview included the dementia patient, Mrs. Thompson, her daughter, Betty Thompson, who was in a wheelchair as the result of a childhood disease, Betty's attendant, and one of Mrs. Thompson's granddaughters. The assessment revealed Mrs. Thompson had severe cognitive deficits. There had been at least a three-year history of symptoms. Betty had brought complete medical and neurological records. Mrs. Thompson's current aberrant behaviors included sorting and resorting her belongings, and wandering. Betty's concerns were whether or not her step-father was doing an adequate job with cooking and cleaning. She also wondered if her mother's problems were due to poor nutrition or to the lack of stimulation due to her stepfather's reclusive lifestyle.

When asked about her mother's nutrition, Betty replied that her stepfather had stocked up on frozen dinners when he had to take over the cooking. Although the counselor stated that frozen dinners were probably nutritionally adequate, Betty was still concerned about their diet. Betty also worried that the care he was providing might not be adequate. It was determined that he was not willing to come for counseling but might attend a family meeting.

**Family Meeting.** The meeting was planned during a counseling session with Betty. She first determined that her stepfather would attend. The location of the meeting presented other problems. Mr. and Mrs. Thompson lived in a rural area 80 miles away. Holding the meeting there would not be convenient for most of the family. Mr. Thompson was willing to drive into the city. As it was a large family (five children and seven grandchildren), there were many possible places to hold the meeting, but Betty said the family was split into two factions which did not get along with each other. Holding the meeting at the home of a person in one faction would cause the other faction to refuse to attend. After discussing this situation with the counselor, Betty noted there was one neutral person who got along with both factions, and it was decided to hold the meeting there.

The meeting itself was quite large. Attending were Mr. and Mrs. Thompson, their five children, four spouses of the children, and seven grandchildren. Two counselors were present, including the one who had conducted the initial assessment and planning with Betty.

When they entered the room, the counselors noted that there was considerable tension, with the two factions seated opposite each other. The counselors observed this arrangement but did not comment on it. They began the meeting by providing information about Mrs. Thompson's illness, pointing out the fact that Mr. Thompson had not caused it by anything he had done. There were several questions about cures that family members had heard about and whether or not it would be worth taking Mrs. Thompson to a new doctor. By providing information from Mrs. Thompson's medical records that indicated prior workups had been thorough, the counselors helped the family decide not to pursue more evaluations. Had the family decided to consult another doctor, the counselors, of course, would have supported that decision as well.

The counselors then moved to discuss methods to solve the problem of care for Mrs. Thompson and to provide relief for Mr. Thompson. Because he had not previously complained, most of the family had not realized the severity of the problem. Having Mrs. Thompson present at the meeting was helpful because it demonstrated to the family that her impairments were great. When he was questioned about what he wanted, Mr. Thompson first said he was managing all right. Then he stated that he would like a few hours off on the weekends to go fishing. Betty then brought up her concerns about their diet, and he admitted he would like some help preparing meals.

At that point, another daughter brought out a calendar and suggested scheduling visits by various relatives so that Mr.

Thompson could go fishing. She said there were five of them (Mrs. Thompson's children), and if they each came once a month, it would not be much of a burden on them. Another daughter responded by reminding the family that Mr. Thompson had done a lot for their mother and for them. He had married their mother when they were teenagers and had helped them through difficult times, treating them as if they were his own children. She asked the group to put aside their differences and see what they could do for him. They then agreed to the schedule for relieving Mr. Thompson on weekends. The family focused next on Mr. Thompson's problems with housekeeping and cooking. Another daughter said she would find a housekeeper and proposed splitting the costs five ways. The other children agreed.

**Followup.** Followup with Betty was made by telephone one week after the family meeting and at three and six month intervals. The arrangements worked out in the family meeting for providing respite and hiring a housekeeper had been successful. After nine months, the original housekeeper left, and Betty called the clinic to get help locating another person. She continued to report that her family was satisfied with these arrangements.

**Discussion.** In retrospect, this family meeting was successful by staying focused on the problem of providing support for the caregiver, Mr. Thompson. First, however, the family had to understand the nature of Mrs. Thompson's problems. Despite their long-standing conflict, the family had good problem-solving skills and could come together around the issue of their mother's dementia. The daughter who scheduled the respite visits was a good organizer, and was instrumental in generating the problem-solving process. At a critical point, another daughter was able to offer support to their stepfather and remind the others of the positive role he had played in their family.

## SUMMARY

Family meetings directly address the issue of providing more support to the primary caregiver. The family is potentially an excellent source of support because it can provide help at odd hours or on weekends, and there is no cost. In many families, emotional ties reduce the burden of providing assistance. Family meetings bring together the key persons who are supportive or potentially supportive of the caregiver. Two counselors generally lead the meeting, providing information and initiating the problem-solving process. They also must identify how the family typically handles problems and any long-standing conflicts which might interfere with problem solving. The counselors want to enhance the family's own problem-solving processes, rather than trying to change long-standing patterns. Family meetings are often successful in helping increase the support the primary caregiver receives and improving everyone's understanding of the illness.

# CHAPTER 8

# SUPPORT GROUPS

Support groups are very popular with caregivers and are now available in many communities. The groups offer many unique benefits, especially in that they allow caregivers to share information with one another and to understand their own experiences better. But we believe that support groups are most valuable when they are part of an overall program, and not merely offered by themselves. Furthermore, as with any group treatment, whether self-help or professional, some people are not helped, or will do better in one-to-one counseling.

The support groups we have run use the stress management model discussed in Chapter 5 and are conducted very similarly to individual counseling. The leaders begin by providing information and answering questions and then proceed to introduce the problem-solving process. The support group, however, adds new dimensions to this approach. The management of problem behavior and increasing social support are enhanced because of the interactions among caregivers, who usually learn more quickly from one another than they do from a counselor. But there is potential both for harm as well as good in groups. The clinician's task is more complicated and demanding. A competent group leader must attend not only to the individual concerns of participants, but also their interactions and their response to the group as a whole. Without the right therapeutic environment, the group can have adverse effects. Anyone who has been in a group where all the members ganged up on one participant, or where the leader singled out one or two persons and reduced them to tears with very personal attacks knows that groups can be dangerous. Group leaders have to be well trained to understand the special characteristics of group interactions and how to create a therapeutic atmosphere. While a complete discussion of how to run groups is beyond the scope of this book, the reader might consult some key sources, including Yalom (1975), Hartford (1971), or Lieberman, Yalom, & Miles (1973).

Three important constructs for understanding how groups work are discussed below: 1. group curative factors, 2. group structure, and 3. group norms. The curative factors are qualities of the group interactions, which result in benefits to clients. Yalom (1975) identifies 11 curative properties, which are shown in Table 8.1. Among the positive features particularly relevant to support groups are imparting information, learning one's problems are not unique (universality), imitative behavior, interpersonal learning, and group cohesiveness, that is, feeling accepted by people who understand the caregiver.

Group structure refers to how the group is organized, how often it meets, where it meets, who attends, and so on. These arrangements affect how participants will interact with each other in the group by making the relationships more intense and exclusive, as when a group meets frequently and does not admit new members, or more diffuse as in a group which meets

**TABLE 8.1.**
Curative Factors in Groups

1. Instillation of hope
2. Universality
3. Imparting of information
4. Altruism
5. The corrective recapitulation of the primary family group
6. Development of socializing techniques
7. Imitative behavior
8. Interpersonal learning
9. Group cohesiveness
10. Catharsis
11. Existential factors

From I.D. Yalom, *The Theory and Practice of Group Psychotherapy.* 2nd ed. (New York: Basic Books, 1975,) pp. 3-4.

monthly and has an open membership. Group norms refer to the explicit and implicit rules that arise out of interactions among participants. Norms influence what participants feel is appropriate to say or do in the group. Some groups, for example, establish norms that value feelings, and everyone is encouraged to express emotions. Other groups may set norms that discourage expression of feelings. The particular norms of a group can promote or inhibit the therapeutic goals of participants. Group members, in turn, may behave in ways that upset therapeutic norms. The challenge for the leader is to promote norms and behaviors that bring out more curative aspects in the group experience.

## CURATIVE PROPERTIES IN SUPPORT GROUPS

The stress-management approach takes on new dimensions in groups, due to the curative properties described by Yalom (1975). In terms of imparting information, there is often a wide sharing of information from printed and informal sources. Caregivers are often the best source of information on how to find good, low-cost in-home help or those doctors that provide special attention to dementia patients and caregivers. With respect to dealing with problem behavior, caregivers suggest alternatives based on their own experience which are often quite creative. Furthermore, caregivers will sometimes try something new if the method is proposed by another caregiver, whereas they might not follow a counselor's suggestion. They also learn by observing how other caregivers respond to various problems. This modeling or "imitative behavior" is an important source of new learning, especially in areas where caregivers previously had difficulty making changes.

One caregiver in a support group had been reluctant to take a short vacation, even though he needed some respite. He struggled through this problem in the group, and finally took the vacation with good results. When the same issue came up for another caregiver in the group, she was able to draw on his experience, and reported that it helped her decide to take time off.

As the example above illustrates, caregivers in a group get the sense of helping and being helped by each other. This support is central to the success of a group. In addition to helping with problem solving, participants have an important role in validating each other's experience. Taking care of a dementia patient can be isolating, and caregivers often feel they are alone in experiencing it. Group members value each other's support because they all have gone through similar circumstances and the thought that others have felt the same way helps. As the following case illustrates, finding out others have had the same reactions and problems as they have had is often helpful.

In the third session of a support group, in which members had been somewhat restrained in their emotional expression up to that point, one man recounted an incident that occurred the previous week which had upset him greatly. He had gotten so frustrated by his wife's behavior that he had put his fist through a wall. He expressed shame over having gotten so upset and wondered if there was something wrong with him. As he told his story, there was a hush in the room. When he finished, it seemed as if the other members gave a sigh of relief. Two others spoke up and said they had similar experiences of getting so frustrated they lost control. They had believed something was wrong with *them*, but hearing the first man's story helped them all realize these were normal frustrations associated with being a caregiver.

One of the most important factors in the success of a support group is cohesion. Yalom (1975) defines cohesion as the degree to which members are attracted to and have a sense of having something in common with others in the group. He believes that the development of this sense of cohesion is critical to the success of a group. Without a feeling of belonging to the group, participants will not benefit much from it. A sense of cohesion develops from positive interactions and from identifying with others who have similar problems. It can be promoted by the leader through the development of positive group norms (see below). A comfortable setting for the group meeting, serving refreshments, and other efforts to make meetings pleasant help to build group cohesion.

As group cohesion develops, participants can be encouraged to make contact with each other outside the group. These informal interactions can provide a very important source of support.

## GROUP STRUCTURE

There are a number of different ways of structuring support groups. They can be open or closed, that is, they may or may not accept new members. They can vary in size. The composition can vary as well. Spouses and children of patients can be placed into separate groups or mixed together in the same group. The format can be unstructured and can include speakers occasionally. Frequency of meetings also can vary.

The way the group is structured will have implications for group interactions. Closed groups will develop more cohesion, but there is likely to be attrition over time as participants decide they no longer need the support or if their relative with dementia dies. The group may eventually become too small (two to four members) to be helpful. Open groups are faced with the problem of integrating new persons into a group where members have already established relationships with each other. It is easy in that situation for the new member to feel isolated or rejected and for the other participants to get impatient as the new member raises issues they had previously resolved. Groups which integrate children and spouses will face more problems developing cohesion, and there may even be conflict between generations on some issues. While the members of different generations can cooperate usefully, our experience has been that over time groups separate into one composed of parents and one of children. With respect to organization, a structured format can provide a lot of information, but participants may not feel free to bring up personal matters. A completely unstructured group may run along erratically without allowing caregivers to resolve important issues.

Another question is whether there should be one or two leaders. In general, we prefer starting a group with two leaders because the interactions can be so complicated that even an experienced leader cannot attend to all the important issues that arise. Gradually, as participants learn the group norms, they can take over more responsibility for running the group, and the second leader may no longer be necessary.

## THE ROLE OF THE LEADER AND GROUP NORMS

The role of the leader or leaders is critical to the success of support groups. As in individual counseling, an important function of the leader of the group is to provide accurate information about medical and nonmedical aspects of senile dementia and to answer questions that group members may have. Providing information is essential soon after the group has been formed or when new members join. Questions about causes and treatment will be frequently asked, even by participants who have had opportunities to ask the same questions in one-to-one counseling. The leader also needs to be able to explain why problem behaviors occur and to help caregivers understand the effects of brain damage on behavior.

Another important role of the leader is to structure the group and to set norms by which it will operate. In addition to when, where, and how long the group will meet, the leader can state that he expects people to come on time and call when they cannot make a meeting. Important interpersonal norms involve confidentiality, being non-judgmental of one another, giving everyone a chance to talk, and avoiding side-conversations while someone else is speaking. While the leader can state these expectations at the outset, participants are likely to need some reminding.

There are many situations in which the leader should intervene to ensure that therapeutic norms of behavior are maintained. This would be necessary when a group member cries, when someone excessively dominates the group; when one participant is overly critical of another; when a member is left out and ignored, and when someone has difficulty participating. In the initial meetings of a group, the leader needs to identify those who have not participated and to bring them into the group's activities. While being quiet can sometimes reflect shyness, it can also indicate distress. The best way for the leader to attend to this possibility is to make sure all group members have a chance to participate at some point during the meeting.

Another consideration is to think about how other group members might be reacting to what is being said. Early in the development of a group, it will become apparent that relatives have symptoms of varying severity. There is always the potential that someone with a relative who is mildly impaired will become disturbed hearing about a patient who has become incontinent or lost the use of speech. The leader should focus on the issue of differences between patients, when it comes up in the group discussion, and help reframe it in a positive way. We usually say that people with mildly impaired relatives can learn from those who have been dealing with the disease longer. At the same time, we emphasize there are considerable individual differences in symptoms and the course of the disease. It is important to take each day at a time, rather than to anticipate the onset of certain symptoms. Group members will sometimes make these statements themselves, or say they wished they had gotten more information sooner, even though hearing about the eventual deterioration of the patient is difficult.

In addition to the severity of the patient's symptoms, there will be other differences among group members that may lead them to believe their situations to be unique and they cannot be understood or helped in the group. When that happens, the leader can point out that, while there are differences in the experiences, there are also similarities the caregiver may have had with those of other group members. The differences do not have to keep anyone from participating or gaining from the group interaction. One mark of a successful group is that members learn to accept their differences, while developing positive feelings for one another.

The following example illustrates how leaders can create norms that either promote positive feelings or cause participants to feel isolated or rejected.

One experienced group leader was attending a support group as an invited speaker. The format of the group was that the leader spoke at a podium in a formal, lecturing tone, and the participants were passive. When the invited speaker encouraged group interaction, one man began talking about his problems and became tearful. The group leader did nothing, and so the invited speaker went over to him, put her arm around him, and said it was okay to cry about these very difficult issues.

It should be apparent that the leader who does nothing in this situation gives participants the impression that it is not acceptable to express painful emotions. Being a caregiver, however, is an emotionally draining experience, and one important function of the group setting is to allow individuals to express this fact so that they do not feel as alone or isolated.

The leader wants to encourage individuals to express their emotions, but that should not be the only focus. While some groups only encourage the expression of feelings, we believe there is much that can be gained by discussing pragmatic concerns as well. Members may have trouble with problem solving, with planning, or with accepting support. Leaders can encourage participants to identify how they might deal with problems more effectively, by providing information, using problem-solving strategies, and by encouraging them to provide support and act as role models for one another.

Actions by some members of a group may threaten therapeutic norms and other participants. When a group member is disruptive in either overt or subtle ways, the leader should intervene to maintain the appropriate behavioral norms perhaps by calling attention to the act in a non-blaming, non-judgmental way, asking for reactions to the behavior from the group, providing suggestions for alternative responses, or, if necessary, taking the disruptive participant aside after the meeting to discuss the problem further.

The following example illustrates the effects of disruptive behavior.

In one on-going support group, two of the women participants had spent the first hour discussing their anger about the disease and how it affected their relationship with their husbands. This was the first time they had really been able to admit being angry, and to see it as a normal reaction. Another woman, who was much younger than the other two, came to the group an hour late and in the middle of the discussion. The men in the group immediately focused their attention on her, and she responded to the discussion by stating that she never got angry, just frustrated. This created a tremendous amount of tension, and the leader tried to encourage a nonjudgmental attitude, thereby validating the important feelings the other women had expressed. At that point, the latecomer added that one of the participants (who did not come that week) had just institutionalized his wife. As there were only five minutes remaining in the session, participants had no time to reflect on this important development.

At the end of the session, all the participants, including the latecomer, were visibly upset. One of the leaders discussed this issue with her after the group, as well as the problems created by her coming late. She interpreted what happened as indicating she was not of value to the group, because she felt left out of the conversation. She was also encouraged to raise her concerns with the group about being left out. She came on time to the next session, and when she brought up her concerns, the group expressed that they really did value her. This was a turning point for her, because previously she had maintained that everything was all right. She now admitted that things were hard for her, too, and was able afterwards to focus more effectively on her own problems.

The example given above also illustrates the importance of following through on issues or problems that were not resolved in previous sessions. Also, the group leader must maintain continuity, even when issues are extremely sensitive. Group members are likely to talk about what happened most recently; they are either unable or unwilling to remember previous discussions. By bringing the group back in a timely fashion to unresolved issues, the leader ensures that members will focus on a problem long enough to make a change, rather than just ventilating feelings.

The group as a whole may ignore or discount what one member says, especially if that person raises issues which are troubling to all of them. The leader can call attention to the issue and encourage the group to discuss it, as is illustrated by the following example.

When a relatively new participant to an ongoing group raised the issue of dating someone else while one's spouse was still alive, the group ignored him as if the comment had not been made and continued on another topic. The leader stopped the group and asked if they heard what the person had just said. There was a brief silence, and then they burst into conversation, saying this concern had been on their minds, too. They then had an animated discussion of the pros and cons of involvement with someone of the opposite sex.

The leader also has to help the group deal with participants who have specific problems dealing with others.

In an early meeting of one group, it became apparent to the leaders that one woman liked to talk a lot and to be the center of attention, but she did not listen to other participants, even when they responded to her. One week she raised an issue that was important to everyone. She said she felt different from the other group members, because her husband was in a nursing home, and their spouses were still at home. The other group members responded immediately, saying how important it was to hear about her experiences, because they knew they might have to face institutionalizing their relative at some time in the future. When they finished speaking, she said again that she did not feel she belonged. At that point, the leader stepped in to remind her what other group members had said, which reassured her, and allowed the group to move on to other issues.

In general, the leader can handle interpersonal difficulties in direct, but gentle ways. Appropriate social behavior should be encouraged without the leader being punitive or condescending. If an extremely disruptive member has to be separated from the group, the leader should discuss this step with that member individually, making sure appropriate referrals for assistance are made. There should also be a discussion with the group to explain why this step was taken.

Caregivers who do not do well in groups are usually those who are extremely self-centered, do not listen at all to others, try to dominate a conversation, or have frequent explosive emotional outbursts. Others are under a lot of stress or are extremely shy or private. They might do better in the group if they are seen first for individual counseling. Caregivers with severe hearing deficits may also present problems for groups.

## WHO SHOULD LEAD GROUPS? PEERS OR PROFESSIONALS?

There is some controversy over who should lead support groups and what sort of training they should have. Support groups were started in reaction to the lack of help for family members. Groups were often initiated and led by family members themselves. Many have been successful in providing support to caregivers, but others unfortunately have not, sometimes due to the leader's lack of experience responding to problems that can arise in groups.

One solution to overcome the failures is to have groups led by trained professionals. That has been our approach, but it should be evident that a professional degree does not guarantee that someone will be an effective leader. Rather than saying that a professional or a peer is best, one needs to evaluate the personal qualities of the leader.

A good leader should try to develop certain helpful qualities such as, ability and willingness to take responsibility for leadership of the group; knowing how to identify serious problems that cannot be handled in the group and to make appropriate referrals; and knowing how to separate one's personal situation from that of group members and refraining from telling others what they should or should not do. In training leaders emphasis should be made on learning about senile dementia and the aging process, a general knowledge of group behavior and leadership strategies, and basic clinical skills, such as the ability to empathize and solve problems.

### CASE EXAMPLE

### Case. A Time-Limited Support Group

The following case study of a support group illustrates many of the principles of treatment discussed previously. The content of the group's activity is based on the stress management model of imparting information and using problem solving to manage the patient and to increase the caregiver's social support. The leaders are active to establish therapeutic norms and to build cohesiveness among members.

This group was formed as part of a research project to determine the effectiveness of support groups. Extensive notes on group sessions had been made by the therapists after listening to recordings of the session. Many of the issues which arose in the group are fairly typical of other groups we have run.

There were several features of the group which were determined by the research protocol and affected its development. One was that caregivers in this group had not been seen by a counselor individually, except for an initial assessment session. Another was that all patients were living at home with the caregiver when the group was started, which would not necessarily be the case in a regular group. Other differences were that this group was closed and time-limited. That is, no new members were admitted after the beginning and the group was scheduled for a specific number of meetings, in this case, seven weekly sessions. Despite these differences, the experiences of the experimental group were similar to those of regular support groups we have led.

A total of eight caregivers were recruited for the experimental group. Other groups in the study ranged between four and nine members, with six to eight considered optimal by the group leaders.

In an initial session caregivers and the dementia patient were seen individually. The caregiver was assessed on his reactions to a number of problems, including the patient's current memory and behavior problems, how the caregiver copes with them, perceived burden, and social support available to the caregiver. Their willingness to participate in the study and to attend the seven sessions was determined. The patient was also assessed to confirm the presence of dementia symptoms. Medical records were obtained to document that the patient had an irreversible dementia, and referrals were made for additional medical assessments if the diagnosis was in doubt.

Characteristics of participants in this group are summarized in Table 8.2. Of the caregivers, four were husbands, three wives and one, a daughter. The latter was the daughter of one of the wives in the group. She lived on the same block as her parents and was involved daily in her father's care. All the other caregivers lived with the patient. The average age of the participants, not including the one daughter, was 68 years. One important feature of this group was that five of the dementia patients currently had severe impairments, as indicated by their inability to get any MSQ items correct. In most groups, patients are not likely to be so impaired.

The group had two leaders, Matt and Linda. Both were experienced in problems of dementia.

**Highlights of Group Sessions.** The highlights of the seven group sessions are presented below. They were selected to illustrate common problems that arise in support groups for caregivers and possible responses by the leaders. Commentary on particular incidents is in bold face.

### SESSION 1.

Attending: All participants were present.

The first session began by having participants introduce themselves and describe their situation a little. During the introductions, Betty, one of the participants, asked if her husband could come into the session. She had brought him to the meeting, saying that she believed he was supposed to attend. The leaders asked the other group members what they thought, and the consensus was that they preferred to have Betty's husband stay outside. They felt they could talk more openly that way. She then expressed concern that he would be bored or wander off. The leaders encouraged her to ask her husband if he minded waiting outside until the group was over. She did that, and came back saying he did not mind, but she checked on him a few times during the course of the group. During the session, she responded to descriptions of problem behaviors by other caregivers by stating that her husband was not that impaired, and she questioned if the group could help her. The group members en-

**TABLE 8.2.**
Characteristics of Group Participants

| Name | Caregiver's Age | Relationship to Patient | How Long Patient Had Dementia | Patient's MSQ score | Major Goals for Group |
|---|---|---|---|---|---|
| 1. Mike | 65 | husband | 3 years | 0 | 1. Learn about financial options; 2. Finding in-home help; 3. Getting time for self; 4. Information about dementia; 5. Support from others. |
| 2. Dave | 72 | husband | 7 years | 0 | 1. Finding in-home help; 2. Getting more family support; 3. Getting time for own activities. |
| 3. Henry | 72 | husband | 5 years | 0 | 1. Support; 2. Managing problem behaviors. |
| 4. Eleanor | 59 | wife | 5 years | 8 | 1. Emotional support; 2. Learning to manage her own anger and depression; 3. Managing her husband's hovering around her; 4. Getting in-home help; 5. Getting time for self. |
| 5. Betty | 74 | wife | 5 years | 6 | 1. How to maximize her husband's abilities; 2. Dealing with his anger; 3. Being patient with him. |

| | | | | |
|---|---|---|---|---|
| 6. George | 70 | husband | 7 years | 0 | 1. Meet others coping with the same problem;<br>2. Time to socialize<br>3. Be able to go away for a weekend;<br>4. Manage his wife's problems better. |
| 7. Jane | 63 | wife | 3 years | 0 | 1. Increase her husband's activities;<br>2. Learn how other people have handled this problem;<br>3. Get out more by herself, do enjoyable things. |
| 8. Sally | 32 | daughter | 3 years | 0 | Not determined |

couraged her to continue coming to the group, and the leaders pointed out there were similarities and differences among all of them, but they still could learn from one another.

Betty's concern about what would happen to her husband is a common one. A major obstacle to support-group participation is that the caregiver often does not have a place to leave the patient safely during group sessions. No provision was made for patients to be watched when this group met, but other caregivers had managed to make arrangements to have their relative supervised. Betty interpreted the program as having been set up for her husband, not herself and that he should be included in the sessions. During the assessment interview, she had been read a standardized description of the program, and signed a consent form, both of which stated the purpose of the program as helping caregivers. Her interviewer did not recall saying anything that would have led her to believe her husband was to participate. The group leaders let the group decide about whether or not her husband should attend and tried to explain their decision so it did not seem they were rejecting Betty. Another group might have decided to include a patient, although most prefer talking without patients present.

The other problem she raised during the session, that her husband's impairment was less severe than others in the group, was an important point. With the exception of Eleanor's husband, all the other patients were severely impaired. A common problem in groups is that caregivers of mildly impaired individuals do not want to hear about more severe problems. This represents a major threat to group cohesion, and the leaders need to establish some issues that participants have in common, despite obvious differences. Without minimizing their individual problems, the leaders want to emphasize the similarities. Unless that can be done, the participants will not view the group as relevant to their situation.

This session was so planned that members of the group would be given the opportunity to ask questions about the disease. After these had been answered, the problem solving was introduced. Caregivers were shown how to keep daily records of problem behavior and were given notebooks with a record for each day until the next group meeting.

Toward the end of the session, several participants complained about not getting enough support from family members. George's family lives out of town and these members are not involved in their mother's care, nor do they provide much emotional support for George. Eleanor felt she got too much support. She believed her daughter thought she was not doing enough, and had been encouraging Eleanor to devote even more time to her husband. At the same time, she was feeling angry and resentful because she felt she was spending too much time with him already. She wanted to decrease her involvement. Mike and Henry also identified family problems. Mike's sister-in-law would not visit anymore, even though they had all been close in the past. One of Henry's daughters was very critical of how he was caring for his wife, although his other children were supportive.

## SESSION 2.

Attending: Mike    Absent: Betty
          Dave             Henry
          Eleanor
          George
          Jane
          Sally

The session began with the group leaders commenting on two members who were not attending the session. Linda had heard from Henry, one of those who was not there, that he had placed his wife in a nursing home after her health had suddenly worsened. He was not able to attend this session, but planned to come to the next. Betty, who had been ambivalent about the group the week before, was not there and had not called. The leaders said they would call her to find out why she did not attend. A couple of the group members said they would call Henry to see if he needed anything.

It is important to call attention to the comings and goings of participants. Persons will miss meetings or drop out. If these changes are not discussed in the group, it can lead to a variety of misinterpretations, such as:

The group is not a good place to get help;
No one has a commitment to come, so why should I take the chance of baring emotions;
We did something to drive that person away.

As a support group develops, participants often take over this function of calling people who do not attend.

The majority of the second session was spent discussing problem solving. The leaders again described how to use the notebooks passed out in the first session for keeping track of problem behavior. They explained how to look for causes and consequences of problems. Linda then asked if anyone had an example from their daily records. Mike brought up how he had used Haldol in the past week to control his wife's restlessness. Linda commented on how the daily records could be used to monitor the effects of drugs and asked if anyone else had experience with Haldol. Dave said his wife had had it prescribed, but there were adverse effects. Linda and Matt then discussed the possible positive and negative effects of drugs and encouraged members to consult their physicians and also to use the daily records to monitor the patient's behaviors as a way of measuring the drug's effects.

The conversation concerning the use of drugs illustrates the importance of following up on a diversion from another type of discussion. Although the leaders had a planned structure and topic for the session, the issue of drugs was clearly on the minds of several participants. Rather than tabling the discussion, the leaders encouraged it. When it was resolved to everyone's satisfaction the leaders took up the discussion of problem solving once again. It is often better to go with an important issue when it is brought up, than to divert it to later in the session. An exception is when someone interrupts an important discussion or conflict that has not yet been resolved to talk about something else, perhaps of less importance. In that situation, the leaders would acknowledge the possible importance of the issue, but bring the group back to the original topic.

Leaders also need to recognize that drugs are a much more attractive solution for everyday problems than is using the problem-solving process. The latter involves much more effort on the part of caregivers. While interventions requiring less effort are desirable, problem solving is necessary if medications do not work effectively, if there are intolerable side effects, or if there are other reasons for not using drugs.

Linda brought the discussion back to the use of daily records. Eleanor said that some relatives came in to stay with her husband on Thursday, and after that, she felt relieved for several days.

She believes that being with her husband all the time makes her tired and stressed, so that she overreacts to little things. By getting temporary relief, she found herself much better able to cope with her husband's problems. The leaders reinforced her use of the records and gave her encouragement to arrange for regular help.

George discussed his wife's incontinence of bowel and his angry reaction to it. He felt ashamed of his anger and believed that he wasn't prepared for her incontinence, which was why he got so angry. Matt also pointed out that George noted on his daily records that he got angry another time when he was tired. Matt responded that it was normal to get upset. Matt inquired about how George had managed urinary incontinence in the past in order to learn to deal with this new problem. The group then discussed possible causes of her incontinence, including a new medication she was taking. Matt brought the discussion back to the factor of fatigue, and George talked about the fact that he was unable to get out often. The group discussed getting out as a means of relieving fatigue.

Jane noted the main problem she had with her husband was restlessness and anger. Walking with him and taking him for drives helped, but she got tired of that and had other things she preferred to do. She also said his behavior was unpredictable when he became angry. Matt inquired about violence or possible danger to Jane, but she said there was none.

When working with caregivers, the practitioner has an obligation to assess the degree of danger in a situation. There will be small numbers of cases where the caregiver could harm the patient and others where the patient presents a danger to the caregiver, as Jane's initial comment implied. The leader cannot ignore the fact that the caretaker or the patient is abusing the other, even unknowingly. When the possibility is raised in a group, the leader can tactfully ask for more information. By phrasing clear, direct questions, the leader can determine the degree of risk to the patient or caregiver. In states with laws prohibiting the abuse of elders, the finding of such acts may require that they are reported to the appropriate public agency.

In reviewing her daily records, Jane thought her husband's restlessness might begin whenever she sat down to rest. The leaders encouraged her to continue to check her daily records and report back next week. Jane also mentioned that something Henry said the previous week had helped her out. He had noted that he thought it was important to take his wife out, and he was not concerned about what other people might think about her odd behavior. Jane said that helped her to take her husband out; it was calming for both of them.

Finally, other members reviewed their daily records. Toward the end of the session, there was a discussion on political activities to support pending legislation in the state legislature which benefitted dementia victims and their families.

## SESSION 3.

Attending: Mike     Absent: Dave
           Henry              Betty
           Eleanor
           George
           Jane
           Sally

Linda began the session by discussing a phone call she had made to Betty. Betty said she did not want to continue with the group because of the difference in the behavior of her husband and the patients of the others in the group. This was discussed, and several members reported how they were finding the group of value. Linda and Matt then passed out information participants had wanted, including phone numbers of service agencies and some recent articles on Alzheimer's disease.

A major focus of the session was Henry's discussion of institutionalizing his wife. The group listened quietly while he described the events leading to his wife's placement, her sudden deterioration in health, emergency admission to hospital, pressure from his doctor and family to place her, his difficulty in making the decision, and the aftermath of institutionalization, which involved feelings of guilt about making the decision. The leaders were supportive and encouraged him to continue talking. He reminisced about the things he had done for his wife while she was at home, and others commented about his good caretaking. He restated that he could no longer physically manage his wife because of her worsened condition and that he had made the best decision he could. He sounded as if he were trying to convince himself that the decision was the correct one.

Matt then tried to involve the group more actively by commenting on the relevance of the decision to institutionalize, that they all were thinking about it in their own ways. Mike voiced concerns about the cost of long-term care. Linda commented on the conflicting emotions the decision could arouse. George said that his friends had suggested he institutionalize his wife, but he was not ready to do so. Henry then talked about some of the positive features of the home he chose. Henry also described how he continued to provide care for his wife. He was now visiting daily and had intervened with the nursing-home staff to arrange for more personalized care. He was trying to keep costs down by bringing prescriptions himself, rather than allowing the nursing home to do that. He expressed the idea, however, that the care and supervision in the home to be good, and felt that gave his wife a feeling of security.

Mike asked if Henry felt some relief that the burden of constant caregiving was over. Henry said he just felt tired. Mike related that to retiring from work. Linda pointed out that the major changes which occurred in his life the last week would make anyone tired. Henry believes he will feel relieved when he thinks his wife has adjusted to the home. Others in the group said they also might feel relief at placement. Eleanor said she thought Henry's wife might feel more secure in the nursing home because of her physical problems, and she also said she felt he was an unusually sensitive caregiver. Linda thanked him for sharing his experience and urged him to continue in the group.

The leaders made the decision to give Henry as much time as he wanted to discuss placing his wife. He was very ambivalent about his decision and was near tears throughout the discussion. For the group to be successful, the leaders needed to communicate acceptance, both of

Henry's decision and his feelings, and to encourage others to express a similar acceptance. The purpose is to create an atmosphere where members can safely talk about deeply felt emotions without fearing criticism or rejection.

The leaders now turned to problem solving. Several of the members reported improvements in the behavior of their relative as a result of applying new approaches thought out through problem solving. George had not lost his temper during the week and had determined to control his wife's incontinence with diet. Jane saw a correspondance between her husband's restlessness and a cold medication he was taking, and she discontinued it. He improved, but is still restless in the late afternoon. Eleanor had gotten someone to come in during the week to stay with her husband and reported feeling more relaxed but still tired. She had also enrolled her husband in day care. Mike also had a less stressful week, which he believes is due to the Haldol his wife is taking, but he had not been successful in involving her in any activities. The meeting ended with Sally commenting on how the caregivers have individual needs. Thus, Henry needs to be very involved in the care of his wife, while Eleanor needs more time away. She observed that recognizing these differences was important and encouraged them to be themselves in providing care to their relative, rather than looking to someone else to tell them what was right or wrong.

## SESSION 4.

Attending: All participants were present.

At the beginning of the session, George passed around a few recent news articles concerning Alzheimer's disease, which he brought in each week. The other members were interested in the articles and often asked for copies.

After looking at the clippings, group members raised several informational questions: What is the duration of Alzheimer's disease? How is the diagnosis made? Why do doctors vary in making the diagnosis? They also discussed upcoming lectures and television programs pertaining to dementia.

The leaders then encouraged a discussion of the results of the caregivers efforts at problem solving. Several members provided updates of their attempts to manage troubling behavior. Dave had experienced the most unsettling problem. He had gone out of town the previous week and had left his wife with their daughter. After going to a restaurant with her daughter, Dave's wife refused to get back into the car to go home. Instead of cooperating, she began accusing her daughter of trying to hurt her and insisted on seeing Dave. They argued for some time, but nothing calmed her down. Instead, she got more and more agitated, until she collapsed and the paramedics were called. Although she had similar episodes of unreasonable behavior in the past, this was by far the most serious.

When Dave arrived home, she continued making accusations against their daughter. Dave tried to reason with her but reported to the group that he had no success. In fact, she denied having done anything wrong, and insisted it was her daughter's fault that she had gotten upset.

Matt tried to present the incident in a different perspective for Dave. He suggested that the behavior was his wife's way of saying she was very upset over his leaving. Matt further suggested that Dave should acknowledge that she was upset, rather than arguing with her about whether she was at fault. Dave noted that when he had empathized with her in other disturbing incidents, it had a calming effect.

A general discussion followed about whether incidents like the one Dave described indicated that the dementia patient was now worse. Matt pointed out that the number of accusations made by dementia patients sometimes decrease as the dementia progresses. Dave remained concerned about the causes. Using the problem-solving method, several possible antecedents for Daves' wife's behavior were explored, including Dave's going away, the fact that his daughter was not informed about the right dosage of medication his wife was to receive, and had not given her the proper dose, and that his wife had an alcoholic drink before lunch and then ate very little lunch. The leaders pointed out that any or all of these events could have triggered the episode. Dave agreed that he would watch in the future to see if he could identify what brings on similar episodes. He also decided to give his wife nonalcoholic drinks, because of the amount of medications she was taking, and its possible role in producing the disturbing behavior.

When Dave first began talking about the incident, he expressed feelings of hopelessness—that his wife had worsened and there was nothing he could do to control her irrational behavior. By reframing the incident as an expression of emotions, rather than a random event, the leaders were giving Dave a way of understanding and responding to his wife's behavior. At the same time, it is important for the counselors to acknowledge and not negate his feelings. The search for antecedents gave him a means of possibly controlling future outbursts. The result was that he gradually felt less overwhelmed and more optimistic. This example illustrates the importance of problem solving, which can lead to something positive caregivers can try to modify troubling situations.

Toward the end of the session, George expressed the opinion that he had not used good judgement in the past week. He cited a recommendation from his doctor that low-stress environments are best for the patient and the caregiver. But he has found that what is low stress for his wife is isolation, and that is *high* stress for him. He has been doing what is good for his wife, and forfeits what he wants, to get out more and socialize. He is reluctant to leave her with anyone, and this is making him tense and angry. He did note, however, that he had a new plan for finding someone to stay with his wife.

Part of his complaint was that his wife does not acknowledge what he is doing for her and is no longer affectionate toward him. Linda commented that her lack of affectionate behavior makes it harder for him to fulfill his commitment to her, and points out how important it is for him to find ways to meet some of his needs.

Eleanor then encouraged George to continue his search for someone to stay with his wife. She recounted how she had someone stay with her husband five days during the past week. She felt good about having done that, saying that having more time off from caregiving allowed her to be more affectionate with him when she was there. Although she was doing better with her husband, her relationship with their daughter remained strained. Her daughter still believes that Eleanor should be around as much as possible, although she is saying she is trying to understand Eleanor's feelings. Linda reinforced this statement as a positive step by the daughter, that she is at least considering Eleanor's perspective. Other group members were very supportive of the arrangement Eleanor had made to get time away. Linda concluded by saying that Eleanor knows she is doing a good job now, that she regrets her daughter does not understand her, but the daughter is now trying to be supportive.

Henry then discussed the problem he was having with one of his children, who was violently opposed to his placing his wife in a home. Picking up on this theme, Sally talked about her experience as a daughter. She identified the process she went through as

1. Thinking the problem would go away;
2. Hoping the problem would get better;
3. Hoping it wouldn't get worse;
4. Accepting and hoping to be able to continue to cope.

She stressed that children need to learn more about the problem and suggested they go to a support group comprised of children.

## SESSION 5.

Attending: Mike      Absent: Dave
        George           Matt
        Henry
        Jane
        Eleanor
        Sally

One of the leaders, Matt, was away for this session. Irene, an experienced leader who was working on the same project, took his place and was introduced to the group.

The discussion first reviewed participants' daily records and attempts to find solutions to problems. George was discouraged again about managing his wife's incontinence and finding someone to stay with her. Eleanor reported on taking her husband to day care for the first time, and said that he looked sad when she left him. This had bothered her. Mike said he had the same feelings when he left his wife for the group. He also noted that he had followed a suggestion the group had made the week before to use paradoxical instructions with his wife, since she tends to do the opposite of what he tells her. Specifically, when she was playing with buttons on her clothing, she would stop if he directed her to continue. Jane's husband was refusing to take his medications. The early discussion also included sharing information about resources and some upcoming lectures about Alzheimer's disease.

Henry reported he was feeling better about having placed his wife in a nursing home. He cited several examples where the facility was meeting her needs, including an incident where she nearly fell, but the staff prevented it. These events confirmed his feeling that he could no longer constantly take care of her. He said he was sleeping better in the past week. Eleanor reminded him of a story he told the week before about how his wife had recited a prayer. Henry had been surprised when she did that because her speech is severely limited. Eleanor said her reciting the prayer indicated her belief that God was in charge. Henry appeared moved by this interpretation.

The events at the fifth session revealed examples in which caregivers directly give positive feedback to one another, in this case, reinterpreting an incident that had puzzled and upset Henry. Her saying the prayer had led him to wonder how much she understood and if she was happy in the nursing home. Eleanor had thought about the incident between group sessions and now shared her reflections with Henry. Providing this type of supportive feedback is one mark of a supportive group, although in some cases it needs to be modeled initially by the leaders.

The leaders should note who gets support from the group and who does not. The person who is not drawing positive comments at all may be putting the other members off in some way. In this group Henry and George got a lot of support, while Mike, who tended to be blunt and unsophisticated and to ramble a bit when he talked, got very little support. The leaders need to consider how to direct support to these people, who otherwise might drop out. A statement made by Mike at the end of this session (see below) clearly indicates he does not feel as much a part of this group as other members do.

A major discussion arose over how caregivers could get time for themselves. Mike said his major problem was that his wife hovered around him and he had no time for himself. Linda asked what would happen if he asked her directly to allow him some privacy. He said that did not work. Eleanor said her husband was able to respond to her request for privacy, but she had difficulty asking. Irene asked if it had always been difficult for her to request time, and she said it had been. She also said she wanted the privacy so she could concentrate on the tasks she had to do, like balancing the checkbook, but she also believed her husband would feel shut out if she went to another room. Jane said she had similar feelings about leaving her husband alone. Irene wondered if Eleanor and Jane generally had trouble asking for things for themselves. Eleanor said she believed she should make up to her husband for what was happening to him. Irene replied by wondering if anyone could possibly do enough. Eleanor also felt the same way and observed she had always tried to do more and more for her husband. The group then discussed how trying to do too much for a relative leads to exhaustion.

Toward the end of the session, Linda turned the attention of the group to the future of the group. In the initial interview and first session, it had been explained that the group was limited to a certain number of sessions (7) but that participants could continue on their own without the leaders, if they chose. Space would be provided for them where they currently were meeting, or they could meet in their homes.

Linda now asked members if they wanted to continue on their own. Mike thought he would go to the support group that had formed in his community. He had the longest distance to travel to attend. George hesitated and then said he did not know. He reported that Eleanor's getting help reminded him that he needs help but is not doing very well to arrange for it. He complained that he forgot things, because there was so much to do. Sally said that George had not been following through on the suggestions the group had made. Linda asked George what he thought, and he related the efforts he had made to find someone to stay with his wife. Linda summarized that it is difficult for him to leave his wife with someone else, and he agreed. He believes his wife is more difficult to manage and that people where he lives do not want to take care of her. Sally raised the question of whether he had tried to get professional help. He described his efforts again. Linda reflected that he felt it was important to find the right person and he agreed. He is also concerned about money, but is encouraged by Eleanor's example. Sally remained insistent that George had not done enough. She observed that every week he complained about the same problem but did not do anything about it. She encouraged him to work at it. The group commented on the effects on his health of trying to provide all the care himself.

Irene asked if George would be willing to take one step and tell the group what that would be. The group offered suggestions which he rejected. Then he came up with his own suggestion— to get someone to stay with his wife for four hours so he could go out to lunch with a friend. Linda encouraged him to follow up on this choice and asked if he had someone to ask to stay with his wife. He did, but Linda and Irene also explored what he might do if that person was not availab.e.

The interchange described above had begun with a fairly strong confrontation as Sally expressed her disappointment with George's efforts to deal with his problems. Rather than letting the confrontation go on, the leaders supported George. At first, Linda agreed with how difficult it was for him to find someone. Then, later, she and Irene helped him problem-solve concerning how to find someone. While the result was the same as Sally intended, it was done more gently. Confrontation may at times be appropriate, but expressions of anger and frustration can get out of hand, frightening the person these feelings are directed towards, as well as other group members who may conclude that the group is not a safe place for expressing emotions. George, who is stiff and reserved, was beginning to withdraw from the interchange, when the leaders intervened.

Henry then came back to the question of whether or not the group should continue. Henry wanted more sessions. Jane said it was quite an experience to be with six or seven relative strangers and to tell her innermost secrets, which she had not even shared with family or friends. At first, she had found this experience depressing because she had not talked about her situation before or heard what other caregivers were going through. Now she believed the support and suggestions were valuable and wanted to continue. Eleanor said she loved the group and appreciated the leadership. Linda advised the group to continue thinking about this issue and to talk about it in the next session.

**SESSION 6.**

Attending: Mike     Absent: Henry
          Jane
          Sally
          Dave
          Eleanor
          George

As in previous sessions, George began by handing out a recent article he had found in a magazine on Alzheimer's disease. Linda asked him whether he had followed through on his plan to get someone to stay with his wife. He said his wife had hurt her ankle, and he talked about his concerns about her condition. Linda came back to the original question, and he replied that he had, indeed, gone out *twice* during the week, although he did not stay long because he was concerned about the sitter's ability to manage his wife. The group expressed their support for his effort. Linda pointed out that if he would plan things in advance, he would be able to get a sitter and get away. He agreed. Linda stressed the need to plan in advance. He also noted that he is talking with a nurse about staying with his wife for a weekend, while he visits his children. This was one of his original goals when the group began.

Many of the participants now had their relatives in day-care centers. Much of the discussion in this session focused on their experiences with day programs. Jane said her husband started going to a day-care center that week, without incident. He attended on Tuesday, and then slept through Tuesday night. On Wednesday, when he did not go to the center, he reverted to his pattern of being agitated in the afternoon and keeping her awake part of the night. Matt and Linda applied problem solving to his restlessness. Her daily records showed he had been calm in the late afternoon on two days, one when he attended day care and the other time when they had an early dinner. They had been out driving and he asked if they could eat. It was two hours before they usually ate, but Jane stopped at a restaurant, and her husband had a sandwich. He was calm the rest of the afternoon. Matt asked if it would be worth trying to move up their dinner hour, and Jane said she would try and report back to the group next week.

Jane then expressed concern that she could not get much information from the day-care staff about how her husband had done. The group encouraged her to ask the staff for more information. She also was not able to enjoy her time off. Linda commented that she would have to learn to enjoy her time, just as her husband would have to learn to adjust to the day care.

Mike has also taken his wife to a day-care program. He is concerned because he does not think she participates in their activities. Linda commented that a major purpose of day care is to relieve the caregiver and provide a safe environment for the impaired person. Sally pointed out that the change in environment can be beneficial and not participating does not necessarily mean dissatisfaction.

One goal of the group had been to identify community resources such as day-care facilities. Group members had gotten information about day-care programs from the leaders and encouraged one another to try the centers. When someone expressed reluctance about using day care, that was usually overcome quickly when another participant commented on how it would benefit both the patient and caregiver. Unfortunately for George, who was having difficulty arranging for time for himself, his wife was too severely impaired for the day-care programs in the area.

Dave was asked if placing his wife in a day care center might help him. There was a program near where he lives, but he is reluctant to take his wife, because they would put her through a battery of medical tests first. Matt encouraged him to call to see if they would accept the records of her recent examination. Dave was also concerned because she had not accepted other activities programs in the past. Linda suggested the group could help in the process. After some discussion of how he could try day care again, Dave said he is learning from the group that caregivers have to be flexible. Mike and Sally encouraged him to try.

Jane observed that Eleanor had been quiet and asked her what she had been thinking. Eleanor said she believes her husband enjoys the day care more than she thought he would but perhaps she had been projecting her own feelings onto him. Dave pointed out the improvement in Eleanor's mood since the group began. She agreed, and said that having at least three hours a day to herself had made the difference.

The group ended with a discussion of whether or not to continue past the next session, but no decision was reached.

The interchanges described above show how this group was building cohesion. The fact that Eleanor had been quiet was now being noticed by other participants, not just the leaders. Similarly, Mike and Sally were encouraging Dave about trying a day-care center. But just as cohesion was building, the group was also faced with the decision about ending, and they could not reach a decision.

### SESSION 7.

Attending: All members were present.

Henry, who had missed the last session, began by talking about his weekend away with his children and grandchildren. This was the first time he had not visited his wife at least once a day. (On most days, he is going to the nursing home twice.) He reported feeling less depressed. He also said that when he came back and visited his wife, he told her in great detail about the weekend. When he finished, she said to him, "You are absolutely magnificent." As he recounted the story, he had tears in his eyes. He found this statement remarkable, because she ordinarily could say so little. He suggested that other members of the group talk more to their relatives, even if they cannot always respond. Dave said that he agreed with Henry's wife. He knew it would be hard for any of them to institutionalize their spouses and he admired Henry's way of handling it. Both he and Sally discussed how important they felt it was to talk more with the dementia patient.

After discussions of recent news articles on Alzheimer's disease, Matt asked about continuing the group. Henry and Dave both wanted to continue. (Eleanor was concerned, because the leaders were not going to continue with them.) Sally disagreed, and thought leaders were not necessary. Dave said there are questions which the group cannot answer by themselves, even though they benefit from the interactions with one another. Eleanor objected to a leaderless group. She felt that the more verbal people would take control. She also did not want a group than involved just "emoting." She wanted to continue looking for solutions to problems. Sally said emoting is sometimes beneficial to the individual and to other group members. She did not want rigid guidelines about how to run the group. Mike agreed, and said the group should be as extemporaneous as possible. There was then a general discussion of the support they received from the group. Mike went off on a tangent about the support he got from his son, and Linda asked how the group could give support to Mike, bringing the discussion back to the issue of how they would continue. She said this was an example of how they could run their own group.

Eleanor was concerned that people would diverge from the point, and never return without leadership. Matt suggested that a person be allowed to diverge and then be brought back to the original topic of discussion. He also mentioned the possibility of choosing someone to moderate the discussions. Mike and Dave liked the idea and suggested George might fill that role. Mike said there would be weeks when one person has more problems than the others and would need more time in a session. He would not object to that. Dave pointed out that Eleanor is often quiet and the group would have to assure she contributed.

Dave asked George's opinion about the group continuing. George said the group had supported him in getting help. He had found someone to stay with his wife while he visited his children. He said this would be the first time in nine years he had been away from his wife overnight. Everyone supported his decision, and Matt suggested he was doing it for his wife as well as for himself because if he did not rest, he would not be able to take care of her much longer.

The group ended with discussions of problem behaviors. The next meeting was to be the final evaluation for the research. At that time they would schedule their next meeting.

Although participants expressed positive feelings toward the group, they were uneasy about changing its format. No leader had emerged from among them. George had been nominated as a moderator, which was somewhat surprising since his mild hearing loss occasionally caused him to misunderstand a conversation. But he had been an important resource for the group, bringing in newspaper and magazine articles regularly. Sally had at times shown good leadership skills, but as the only daughter in the group, she had not discussed her own situation as much as others and had announced that she was not going to continue with the group. The leaders, although they initially felt that the group could go on by itself, now had some misgivings about the group's ability to continue on its own. It should be noted that the uncertainty about whether or not the group would continue had a depressing effect on participants' mood in this last session.

## OUTCOME

Most of the group did continue meeting, but they did not assume the leadership. Through their urging, Linda agreed to continue to head the group. Mike and Dave, who lived the farthest, did not attend after the last research session. Sally also did not continue, saying that she had gotten sufficient understanding of her father's problems. The other members continued to attend meetings twice a month for the next year. They were joined by caregivers who had attended other groups in the same research project. While the group members were probably not ready to assume leadership themselves after the initial seven sessions, they were virtually running the groups themselves by the end of the year, and Linda assumed a less active role.

Individual outcomes are summarized in Table 8.3. The caregivers were asked to evaluate the extent to which they met the goals they expressed when they first joined the group and to rate their overall situation. Most of the responses indicated the group had a mildly positive effect.

**TABLE 8.3.**
Group Members' Ratings of Outcome

| Name | Goal | Rating Very Much Worse | Some-what Worse | A Little Worse | No Differ-ence | A Little Better | Some-what Better | Very Much Better |
|------|------|------|------|------|------|------|------|------|
| 1. Mike | 1. Learn about financial options | | X | | | | | |
| | 2. Finding in-home help | | | | | | X | |
| | 3. Getting time for himself | | | | | | X | |
| | 4. Information about dementia | | | | | | | X |
| | 5. Support from others | | | | | | | X |
| | 6. Overall rating | | | | | X | | |
| 2. Dave | 1. Finding in-home help | | | | | | X | |
| | 2. Getting more family support | | | | | | | X |
| | 3. Getting time for own activities | | | | | X | | |
| | 4. Overall rating | | | | | | X | |
| 3. Henry | 1. Support | | | | | | | X |
| | 2. Managing problem behavior | | | | | | | X |
| | 3. Overall rating | | | | | X | | |
| 4. Eleanor | 1. Emotional support | | | | | X | | |
| | 2. Learning to manage her own anger and depression | | | | | X | | |
| | 3. Managing her husband's hovering | | | | | X | | |
| | 4. Getting in-home help | | | | | X | | |
| | 5. Getting time for self | | | | | | X | |
| | 6. Overall rating | | | | | | | X |

5. George
   1. Meet others coping with the same problem
   2. Time to socialize
   3. Be able to go away for a weekend
   4. Manage his wife's problems better
   5. Overall rating

6. Jane
   1. Increase her husband's activity
   2. Learn how other people have handled this problem
   3. Get out more by herself, do enjoy-
   4. Overall rating

Note: No outcome data was available on Betty, who only attended the first session. Research data was not obtained on Sally, since the protocol involved taking only one caregiver per family.

Probably the most dramatic changes in the group were shown by Eleanor. She had been quiet and anxious in the first sessions, but gradually talked about her concerns. The group then served as an impetus for her to get in-home help and eventually to take her husband to a day-care center. The group's role was critical because her daughter was pressuring her to spend *more time* with her husband. Gradually, she was able to change her daughter's opinion as well. She gained the assurance that she could ask for a certain amount of time to herself each day. She now understood that without that time she could not effectively care for her husband the rest of the day. Furthermore, she no longer viewed this need for time to herself as a weakness, and was more positive about how she evaluated her caregiving.

Dave and Henry both rated their experiences very positively. Dave had not been as active as other participants, but seemed to gain from the experience. Henry received complete support from the group concerning his wife's placement.

Jane was the only participant who rated her situation as somewhat worse. Her husband had become increasingly restless and difficult to control during the last few weeks the group had been meeting. The success of problem solving had only short-term results in controlling his agitation. He was also refusing to take medication. Jane had become a good problem solver, but she had not been able to find more time for herself.

For Mike, the outcome was also mixed. He had used problem solving the least; instead he kept hoping that his wife's problems would be controlled by medication. He was also looking for information about how he could pay for nursing homes. The information that he obtained, that there is no Medicare or other insurance coverage until the couple deplete their resources, was depressing to him.

George rated his situation as slightly improved, and he had, in fact, taken some important steps to getting help. He moved quite slowly, however, and waited until the strain was almost unbearable. He had a difficult time applying straightforward suggestions; sometimes he simply ignored them.

## SUMMARY

Support groups provide new opportunities to apply the stress-management method of treatment, although they place considerable responsibility on group leaders. Leaders must be able to develop and maintain therapeutic conditions in their groups. This requires knowing what curative properties are potentially present in groups, how to structure groups, and how to set appropriate group norms. The leaders must mediate conflict among group members and respond to behavior that threaten the norms. While an effective group involves a considerable amount of freedom for the participants to help each other, this process is facilitated when therapeutic norms and procedures are established.

# CHAPTER 9

# SPECIAL TREATMENT ISSUES

This chapter will focus on four treatment issues that have not been addressed in detail in previous chapters. Questions about the use of medications with dementia patients come up quite frequently in working with caregivers, and the section that follows provides basic information on drug usage and side effects. While previous chapters have emphasized the role of families in providing care, the dementia patient occasionally will have no one to step into the caregiving role. The possibilities and limitations in this situation will be discussed. The third issue discussed is how to communicate optimally with dementia patients. Finally, while interventions are intended to maintain patients in their home, nursing-home care may become necessary. How to work with families around the question of placements and some issues of appropriate nursing home care are presented.

## DRUGS AND DEMENTIA

Medications can be an important part of the overall treatment plan for dementia patients. As has been apparent from many of the examples in preceding chapters, however, adverse reactions to drugs are quite common. The reason for this problem is the effects of medications on the behavior of dementia patients are poorly understood. Table 9.1 provides a list of drugs which are prescribed for dementia patients. The intended effects are described, as are adverse effects and other features of the medica-

**TABLE 9.1.**
Drugs Used For Symptomatic Treatment of Dementia

| DRUG<br>Generic Name<br>(BRAND NAME) | DOSAGE<br>RANGE<br>(mg/day) | PURPOSE | ADVERSE EFFECTS | COMMENTS |
|---|---|---|---|---|
| *MAJOR TRANQUILIZERS* (NEUROLEPTICS) | | Control agitation, irritability; clarify thought; improve self-care, cooperation, sociability | Drowsiness; postural hypotension; anticholinergic effects (dry mouth, blurred vision, constipation, urinary retention, tachycardia); extrapyramidal reactions (akathisia (restlessness with agitation and pacing), parkinsonism); tardive dyskinesias; precipitation of seizures in those with seizure disorders. | Low doses are generally effective for patients with dementia.<br><br>Some adverse effects are more common with certain drugs than with others.<br><br>All agents are very long acting and may be dosed once daily. |
| *Phenothiazines*<br>Chlorpromazine (THORAZINE) | 10–400 | | More drowsiness, hypotension, anticholinergic effects, low EPS | Highly sedative agents may increase confusion in some patients. |
| Thioridazine (MELLARIL) | 10–400 | | Highly sedative, hypotensive, most anticholinergic, least EPS | |
| Mesoridazine (SERENTIL) | 10–400 | | High sedation, moderate anticholinergic effects, moderate hypotension | |

| Drug | Dosage (mg) | Effects | Notes |
|---|---|---|---|
| Fluphenazine (PROLIXIN, PERMITIL) | 0.25–5 | High extrapyramidal symptoms (EPS), low sedation, low anticholinergic effects | |
| Perphenazine (TRILAFON) | 2–32 | Low to moderate sedation, high EPS | |
| Prochlorperazine (COMPAZINE) | 5–40 | Moderate sedation, high EPS | |
| Trifluoperazine (STELAZINE) | 2–20 | Moderate sedation, high EPS | |
| *Thioxanthenes* | | | |
| Chlorprothixene (TARACTAN) | 10–100 | High sedation, high anticholinergic effects, low to moderate EPS | |
| Thiothixene (NAVANE) | 1–20 | Low sedation, high EPS | |
| *Butyrophenone* | | | |
| Haloperidol (HALDOL) | 0.5–8 | Low sedation, high EPS | Confusion sometimes seen with this drug. |
| *Dibenzoxapine* | | | |
| Loxapine (LOXITANE) | 10–60 | Moderate sedation and anticholinergic effects, high EPS | Chemically related to doxepin. |
| *MINOR TRANQUILIZERS (ANXIOLYTICS)* | | Reduce agitation, treat insomnia, anxiety | Paradoxic excitation may be seen with all of these agents |
| *Benzodiazepines* | | Oversedation, ataxia, dizziness, fatigue | Long-acting agents may build up in the body, causing a chronic overdose. |
| | | | Long-acting agents have active metabolites. |

**TABLE 9.1.** (Continued)

| DRUG<br>Generic Name<br>(BRAND NAME) | DOSAGE<br>RANGE<br>(mg/day) | PURPOSE | ADVERSE EFFECTS | COMMENTS |
|---|---|---|---|---|
| *Long-acting* | | | | All long-acting agents may have metabolism slowed by cimetidine (TAGAMET) |
| Chlordiazepoxide (LIBRIUM) | 5–20 | | | Duration of action up to more than 100 hours |
| Clorazepate (TRANXENE) | 3.75–15 | | | Active drug is diazepam |
| Diazepam (VALIUM) | 2–20 | | | Duration of action up to 100 hours |
| Flurazepam (DALMANE) | 15 | | Hangover effect when used for sleep | Generally used as sedative-hypnotic |
| Prazepam (CENTRAX) | 10–15 | | | Not intended for routine use |
| *Short-acting* | | | | Most short-acting agents do not have active metabolites, nor have their metabolism slowed by cimetidine |
| Alprazolam (XANAX) | 0.25–0.75 | | | |
| Halazepam (PAXIPAM) | 20–80 | | | |

| Drug | Dose | | | |
|---|---|---|---|---|
| Lorazepam (ATIVAN) | 0.5–4 | | | Cases of retrograde amnesia in elderly have been reported |
| Oxazepam (SERAX) | 10–60 | | | Slow onset of action; commonly used in elderly |
| Temazepam (RESTORIL) | 15–30 | | | Indicated for insomnia |
| Triazolam (HALCION) | 0.125–0.25 | | | Very rapid onset, short duration. |
| | | | | Overdose occurs at four times the maximum recommended dose. |
| *ANTIDEPRESSANTS* | | Treat depression, useful for concurrent insomnia if most or all of dose is given at bedtime. | Anticholinergic effects; sedation; fine tremor; confusion; cardiac effects (arrhythmias, heart block, bundle branch block) | Must be used cautiously in dementia patients<br><br>High risk of overdose, possibly fatal. |
| Desipramine (NORPRAMIN, PERTOFRANE) | 25–100 | | Low sedation and anticholinergic activity | "Low" anticholinergic activity is comparable to that of major tranquilizers with moderate to high activity. |
| Imipramine (TOFRANIL) | 25–100 | | Moderate sedation and anticholinergic activity | |
| Trimipramine (SURMONTIL) | 25–100 | | Highly sedative, moderate anticholinergic activity. | |
| Amitriptyline (ELAVIL, ENDEP, AMITRIL) | 25–100 | | High sedative, anticholinergic, cardiac effects | May be poor choice for most older patients |

**TABLE 9.1.** (Continued)

| DRUG<br>Generic Name<br>(BRAND NAME) | DOSAGE<br>RANGE<br>(mg/day) | PURPOSE | ADVERSE EFFECTS | COMMENTS |
|---|---|---|---|---|
| Nortriptyline (AVENTYL, PAMELOR) | 10–50 | | Moderate sedation, low anti-cholinergic activity | |
| Protriptyline (VIVACTIL) | 5–20 | | Low sedation, moderate anti-cholinergic activity | Monitor cardiac status closely |
| Doxepin (ADAPIN, SINEQUAN) | 10–100 | | High sedative and anti-cholinergic activity | May also have some neu-roleptic activity |
| Amoxapine (ASCENDIN) | 25–150 | | High sedative and anti-cholinergic activity; possible EPS; psychotic reactions; parkinsonism | Shows some adverse effects generally associated with neuroleptics. |
| Maprotoline (LUDIOMIL) | 25–75 | | High sedation; low anti-cholinergic activity; anxiety; agitation; reduced seizure threshold | Reported to have among the lowest anticholinergic activity of the antidepressants<br><br>Unique chemical structure (tetracyclic) |
| Trazodone (DESYREL) | 50–150 | | High sedation; very low anti-cholinergic activity | Least anticholinergic<br>Low incidence of cardiac effects |
| Nomifensine (MERITAL) | 25–100 | | Very low sedative, anti-cholinergic and cardiac effects | Newly released in USA. Very little clinical data yet available |

## OTHER AGENTS

| | Dosage | Action | Side effects | Comments |
|---|---|---|---|---|
| Vasodilators | | Improve cerebral blood flow and thus oxygen supply to brain | | Alzheimer's Disease is not a vascular problem. These drugs have little or no effect on sclerotic vessels. Not specific for cerebral vessels, may shunt blood away from involved areas |
| Cyclandelate (CYCLOSPASMOL) | 200–800 | | Gastrointestinal disturbances, headache, tingling, weakness, flushing, tachycardia | Of doubtful value |
| Isoxsuprine (VASODILAN) | 40–80 | | Dizziness, hypotension, tachycardia | Of doubtful value |
| Niacin (NICOBID) Nicotinyl Alcohol (RONIACOL) | not established 50–300 | | Flushing of face and neck, gastrointestinal disturbances, tingling, itching | Vitamin Of doubtful value |
| Papaverine (PAVABID) | 90–300 | | Nausea, anorexia, anticholinergic effects, abdominal discomfort, dizziness, headache, facial flushing | Efficacy of this drug has never been documented in controlled clinical trials. |
| *Metabolic enhancers* | | Stimulate brain metabolism and thus improve memory | | |

**TABLE 9.1.** (Continued)

| DRUG<br>Generic Name<br>(BRAND NAME) | DOSAGE<br>RANGE<br>(mg/day) | PURPOSE | ADVERSE EFFECTS | COMMENTS |
|---|---|---|---|---|
| Ergoloid mesylates<br>(HYDERGINE, DEAPRIL-ST) | 3-6mg | | Transient nausea, gastric disturbances, vomiting, sublingual irritation | Controversial<br><br>Few good clinical trials published<br><br>Of questionable value at recommended dosage |
| *Choline derivatives*<br>Lecithin | not established | Supply acetylcholine precursors for enhanced activity in the brain | Nausea, gastrointestinal upset, diarrhea | Of questionable value, as access to the central nervous system is minimal |
| Physostigmine<br>(ANTILIRIUM) | not established | Supply acetylcholine precursors for enhanced activity in the brain | Bradycardia, salivation, emesis, urination and defecation | As yet unproven. Risk of anaphylactic reaction makes use dangerous.<br><br>Must be injected. |

Prepared by Bradley R. Williams, School of Pharmacy, University of Southern California, Los Angeles.

tions. The list has been organized into major classes of drugs, including major tranquilizers, minor tranquilizers, antidepressants, and other compounds which are frequently used. Characteristics of specific drugs within each class are then briefly described.

The drugs most commonly used are major tranquilizers such as Haldol (haloperidol), Mellaril (thioridazine), Thorazine (chlorpromazine), and Navane (thiothixene). They are typically prescribed to reduce agitation, restlessness, angry outbursts, and insomnia. The patient's response to these drugs can vary considerably. Some patients do well on low dosages for extended periods of time. Others show no response, and increasing the amount only makes problem behavior worse or introduces new problems. Still others produce an immediate negative response. Patients may become extremely agitated, restless, or begin hallucinating. These responses are paradoxical, that is, opposite to the intended effects of the medications. In our experience, paradoxical reactions are common with dementia patients. Frequently these drugs will have beneficial effects for a period of time but then the problem behavior becomes worse. Increasing the dosage at that point often exacerbates the problems. Lowering or eliminating the drugs may have beneficial effects. It is important to understand that the positive effects of any drugs can be short-lived, and the drugs can cause undesirable effects.

A variety of other drugs are sometimes prescribed for symptoms associated with dementia, including antidepressants, minor tranquilizers, and vasodilators. These medications can have a variety of adverse effects, which range from drowsiness to increased mental impairment to severe physical damage (e.g., tardive dyskinesia).

When a medication is causing a negative effect, changes in the dosage or stopping it entirely will not have immediate beneficial effects. Because the drugs have built up in the patient's body, they will continue to influence behavior for some time, perhaps as long as a month. Furthermore, changes must be made under a doctor's supervision, because too sudden withdrawal can cause other adverse reactions.

Certain procedures can maximize benefits and minimize the potential for negative effects of a new medication. As with any intervention, the medication needs to be viewed as an experiment. The first step is to be fully informed about the possible side effects of the drug, and identify other problems to look for, such as paradoxical reactions. With this in mind, families can monitor the behavior that the drugs are intended to control. Daily records of behavior are the best way to determine what effects the medications are having. If these records show worsening of problems, or the appearance of new problems, that is evidence that the medications may not be having their intended effect.

It is also important for families to know that the tranquilizing drugs are not treatments for the underlying disease. Their role is to control problem behavior, and if they do not do that, there is no reason to continue their use.

Obtaining cooperation of a prescribing physician is important. Because physicians are not in frequent contact with the patient, and do not observe daily behavior, they sometimes view medication reactions as part of the disease process. This situation is frustrating for families. Good care for dementia patients depends on identifying physicians who are well informed about the use of drugs in dementia patients. Clinical pharmacists are also knowledgeable about these medications and can be valuable in planning and evaluating drug regimens.

## PATIENTS WITHOUT FAMILIES

When the dementia patient has no immediate family, or a family which refuses to get involved, maintaining the patient in the community is more difficult. Community agencies usually cannot assume the responsibility of daily maintenance and supervision of the patient. Through a case coordination approach, however, practitioners can function in the capacity of advocate, seeking out the best care available to maintain the person in the least restrictive setting.

Obtaining assistance for an isolated dementia patient can be very difficult. Service providers will encounter a tremendous amount of prejudice against these patients and lack of knowledge about dementia among personnel of social and health agencies. Complicating the situation are inconsistent and confusing regulations for reimbursement of community services under Medicare and Medicaid (Medi-Cal in California). Many of the people who are asked for help are likely to say: "Just put the patient in a nursing home." But practitioners have the responsibility to do what patients want. If their preference is to stay at home, then that should be attempted first. Home care may be possible if supportive services can be arranged. We believe it is our obligation to explore the possibility of home care, and only to turn to nursing homes when that proves impossible.

When there is no family, alternative sources of assistance may be available. Service providers can inquire among the patient's friends, neighbors, or church to determine their willingness and ability to take on some of the responsibilities for care or supervision. Even if individuals are only able to give a small amount of their time, that may be useful in building a support system. The practitioner will want to educate these helping persons about dementia and how they can best respond to the patient.

A major limitation in case management is that arranging the needed combination of informal and formal services can be time-consuming. It is not just a matter of making a few phone calls to obtain services. Rather, the practitioner plays the roles of educator and advocate. With high case loads, practitioners may not have the time for effective case coordination. Case management models need to address the problem of how much time is involved when a client has dementia.

Examples of home care for dementia patients and other frail elderly can be found in the book *Creative Mental Health Programs for the Elderly* (Glasscote, Gudeman, & Miles, 1976). British programs described in that book provide an integrated program of in-home and community services which make it possible for many elderly who might otherwise be institutionalized to continue residing at home.

## RELATING TO DEMENTIA PATIENTS

Many of the suggestions in previous chapters for managing problem behavior have involved changing the typical way family members relate to the dementia patient—empathizing with a patient rather than arguing with him or her. Sometimes families and service providers assume they have to change everything about the way the caregiver relates to the patient. They overgeneralize the effects of the brain damage by treating patients as if they were children, talking in front of them as if they were not there, talking loudly as if they were deaf, or taking away tasks they can still do for themselves.

Patients sometimes act in childlike ways or are seemingly unaware of conversations around them. But they vary in the extent of their awareness and will often be more aware of what is being discussed than they indicate. In one instance, an inexperienced student was advising the wife of a dementia patient while he was present that she needed to put him in a nursing home. The student assumed the man could not understand and treated him as if he was not there. Although this patient was severely impaired in understanding and speaking, he became visibly upset during this conversation and remained so for several days. This variability in understanding is common, even in the most severely impaired individuals.

The most important consideration in relating to dementia patients is to treat them with dignity. Even when they do not understand or respond, it is better to assume they understand at least something about the situation. They may respond to the emotional connotations of a situation, rather than the overt. But in this way they do maintain some relationship to their family. Often, patients appear to know the attitudes of people who interact with them, whether those people are friendly or hostile, sympathetic or angry.

Sometimes dementia patients have an awareness of their problems or express interest in talking to a counselor. Brief counseling sessions may be helpful in alleviating some of the depressive affect that accompanies the dementia, especially in its earlier stages.

## WHEN NURSING HOMES ARE NECESSARY

The issue of when and if nursing-home placement is appropriate will come up in virtually every case. While in-home and community care has been emphasized, nursing homes are an important option that should be discussed with families so that they can plan for every possibility. Giving families permission to talk about nursing-home placement helps put it in a realistic perspective. Rather than saying relocation to a nursing home is necessary, we help the family view it as one of the alternatives available to them. As with other possibilities, placement has positive and negative aspects. When family members are under stress, there is a temptation to view nursing homes as a means to relieve all of their burden. But if they have the opportunity to investigate that option for themselves, they will often see the limitations as well as the advantages of nursing-home care.

The best way to help with the decision of whether or not to relocate a patient is to train families to become good judges of services. This involves articulating their expectations of a nursing home, shopping for facilities which accept dementia patients, and talking with families who have placed patients in nursing homes. They need to evaluate quality of care, not just the physical facilities. Some ways of evaluating quality include staff-patient ratios, staff turnover, and the staff's knowledge about dementia. Families can go to the administrator with a list of questions of how the nursing home would respond to problems their relative has, such as incontinence or wandering. They can ask what the nursing home does to help brain-damaged patients adjust to a new environment and about on-going programs of in-service training for staff, especially pertaining to dementia. Of course, families can review the latest state reports available at a facility that evaluate compliance with state and federal regulations.

When families have had the opportunity to explore all of the options available, they can place their relative under institutional care knowing they have done everything they can. Some family members will still feel guilty about the decision, but they can be reminded they have done the best they could. Sometimes caregivers have resolved they would never put anyone in a home, and they feel especially bad when they are forced to do so. It can be pointed out, however, that when the resolution was made, they did not anticipate anything as catastrophic as dementia.

Once placement is made, family members may find it unpleasant to visit their relative. Service providers need to stress the importance of staying involved. Even if patients do not respond or are angry with family members, visits are still important to them. Family members can also be advocates for their relative, ensuring that the quality of care is as good as possible.

While we have stressed home care throughout this book, there is a role for nursing homes in an ideal community-oriented system. One important function is to provide respite care, such as is available in Great Britain. Respite care enables families to leave their relative in the nursing home for however long they need to get relief from the daily burdens of care. Families we have worked with say that respite care is the service that would help them the most and in some instances would have alleviated the need for permanent nursing-home placement. Other functions include taking over when the patient's impairments are too great for the family to manage or when no informal supports are available.

There has been surprisingly little attention paid to the specific problems and needs of dementia patients in institutional settings, although recently both advocacy groups and the industry itself have begun to look at this issue. However, the research literature currently available provides few guidelines as to what type of programs or environment is best (Zarit & Anthony, 1985). Many studies which purport to include dementia patients usually have ignored anyone who was troublesome, forgetful, or could not cooperate with the research. Other studies were made without adequate control groups. The literature on reality orientation is a good example of this problem. While reality-orientation classes, in which patients are reminded what day it is and where they are, have been shown to have generally positive effects, they have not been compared to other types of treatment. This absence of suitable control groups makes evaluation of these programs difficult. It is not clear if benefits are due to reality-orientation techniques or to increased stimulation that patients could receive in any number of other ways.

In current discussions of institutional care of dementia patients, the most important question to answer is whether or not there should be separate facilities for dementia patients. In many parts of the country, there is a clear need for *more* beds for dementia patients whether they are separated or not. Families who want to place a patient often cannot find a nursing home that will take a dementia patient, especially one who wanders or is otherwise difficult to manage. Placement can be extremely difficult to arrange if the patient is on Medicaid. The one alternative that is readily available is locked facilities for the care of chronic mental patients. While this type of institution sometimes provides good care, it is often unacceptable to families who would prefer to see their relative in a special Alzheimer or dementia unit.

Special dementia units have been established in some of the European countries and in Canada, and are now being developed in the United States. These facilities are often designed to accommodate the problems caused by dementia. They may, for example, have a secure environment that allows wandering patients to roam without risk of injury, or have flexibility in the daily routine so that patients who cannot conform to a schedule may eat or sleep when they wish. The staff of these facilities often receive special training that includes techniques for calming patients with soothing words, with touch or attention, instead of drugs or restraints. The combination of a well-designed environment and good staff training can make it possible for patients to be maintained on drug-free regimens or on lower dosages than are typically found in nursing homes. In fact, the behaviors that typically lead to overuse of physical or chemical restraints, wandering, staying awake at night, or combativeness when the staff tries to enforce rules, can largely be avoided.

A controversial aspect of special dementia units is that they may become places which are stigmatized in the way mental hospitals were in the past. While interest in special units is currently high, public support may become limited as a result. The most realistic prediction is that a few model facilities will be developed which serve private pay clients, but the majority of nursing homes which depend on public sources of reimbursement will have difficulty mounting good programs.

Special units may also be damaging to the patients themselves. That is, someone with mild cognitive impairments may, in fact, benefit from interactions with persons who do not have dementia. Isolating that person in a dementia unit could have a detrimental effect. However, the presence of dementia patients on wards with older patients who are cognizant of their situation and surroundings is often disturbing to the latter group. One approach is to move patients from one ward or facility to another, depending on the care they need. This approach, however, introduces new problems, because of the difficulty dementia patients have in adjusting to new environments.

Another major issue is the purpose of the institution. We currently think about care as a medical problem, and medical institutions have specific regulations and staffing patterns. But most of the time, the care that dementia patients require is not medical, but social. The ideal situation would be to design special environments which minimize the patients' problems and disabilities and to hire staff who can respond with warmth and tolerance to the cognitively impaired patient. Yet a social model might not have the prestige of medical care, nor provide the reimbursement that comes with it.

## SUMMARY

This chapter has touched upon four critical issues in the care of dementia patients. Medications, while sometimes beneficial, can have negative consequences and must be monitored carefully. If patients do not have involved family members, the possibility of providing home care becomes more difficult. When relating to the dementia patient, service providers and family members should treat them with dignity. It is important to give them the benefit of doubt when it comes to understanding what is said or done for them. Patients may also sometimes benefit from supportive counseling. Finally, nursing-home care should be discussed as one option with families. Families can be assisted to be good judges of nursing homes and in continuing to have positive involvements with their relative after placement. There is likely to be increasing emphasis on special dementia units, although their benefits have not been determined.

# CHAPTER 10

# DIRECTIONS FOR THE FUTURE

The major hope for the future concerning the dementias is the discovery of a prevention or treatment. Research efforts toward that end deserve support, and families are often willing to cooperate with researchers. One important way to support research is to arrange for a post-mortem donation of brain tissue from afflicted persons. Because animals do not develop Alzheimer's disease, the primary way of studying it is to use samples of the human brain. Tissue samples obtained post-mortem from Alzheimer's patients are the foundation of basic research on dementia and it is from these studies that advances in diagnosis and treatment can be expected. Arrangements to participate in an autopsy program are often overlooked while the patient is alive, but preparations have to be made well in advance. Although some families may have hesitations about autopsy, the value is unquestionable.

Recently, five major centers for Alzheimer's disease research have been established through grants from the National Institute on Aging. These centers are located at Harvard University, Johns Hopkins University, Mount Sinai Medical Center in New York, University of California at San Diego, and University of Southern California. Families wanting to learn more about current research on Alzheimer's disease or wishing to participate in ongoing studies are encouraged to contact one of those centers, or any of the other universities or medical centers where research on the dementias is being conducted. Information about current research can also be obtained from the National Institutes of Aging and of Mental Health.

The expectation of a cure at some point in the future should not overshadow the way in which care of afflicted individuals is presently given. Unlike the search for a cure, which involves scientific research, issues of care are a political problem of how valuable resources are allocated. Even if a treatment for Alzheimer's disease were discovered tomorrow, many of the same issues of long-term care would remain for other mentally and physically frail elderly, as well as for brain-damaged adults who have some of the same problems as dementia patients. Changes we could make today in the politics of care would result in immediate benefits to families and afflicted individuals.

The major political question is third-party payment of services. The primary health insurance available to the elderly are Medicare and Medicaid (Medi-Cal in California). Medicare, which promises comprehensive health coverage for the elderly, is restricted regarding care of dementia patients. Any type of supportive services which might benefit the patient or family will not be reimbursed. Services such as homemakers, in-home nursing, day care, and even nursing-home care are available to older persons with other medical problems, but the patient suffering Alzheimer's disease or another type of dementia is excluded. The effect of these policies is to drain the family's financial and physical resources, forcing them to place the patient into a nursing home. Typically, Medicaid will assume payment for care only when the family has depleted their personal assets paying for the cost of the nursing home. Families get help, therefore, at the point that they have become paupers. Given the federal and state budget cuts in recent years, even the continuation of Medicaid reimbursement is in question. We may be facing a situation in the near future where all long-term care options are closed to dementia patients.

The new D.R.G.'s (Diagnostically Related Groups) issued by Medicare are potentially of little help for families of dementia patients. The idea of the D.R.G.'s is that hospitals will be reimbursed for the average cost of care for a patient with a particular disease. Under this system, hospitals save money if a patient has a shorter stay than average, and they lose money if the patient stays longer. They also save money if the patient does not require a lot of time from a specialized staff. There is no provision in the D.R.G.'s for reimbursing hospitals to a greater extent if other factors, in this case, dementia, complicate the course of treatment of acute medical problems. Because of their behavioral and cognitive deficits, dementia patients are more difficult to manage in acute hospitals, and their care is probably more costly. It is possible they may come to be viewed by hospitals as particularly undesirable patients. There is the potential for abuses such as discharging these patients prematurely, or pressuring physicians not to admit dementia patients.

More financial support for medical, community, in-home services, and residential care for dementia patients and other individuals with similar debilitating conditions is clearly needed. But in an economy where health-care costs have already been rising much faster than the cost of living, this additional money will not readily be allocated. If one believes that basic supportive services ought to be available, then difficult political questions must be faced. The money would have to come either from higher taxes, from reallocation of resources from another part of the economy, or from a redistribution of current health-care expenditures. None of these prospects is likely without significant changes in the current political climate.

As professionals involved in the care of dementia patients, we have found present policies too constraining to fulfill our obligations to patients and believe it is necessary to support policy and legislation which will make available the right sort of help. In this era of special-interest groups, advocates for dementia patients must organize and skillfully lobby at the state and federal level.

One strategy is to organize a lobbying group around a single disease, such as has been done to some extent for Alzheimer's disease. Historically, interest groups have mobilized support for research to overcome specific diseases (such as cancer and diabetes). With the emergence of the Alzheimer Disease and Related Disorders Association, a similar effort is being made for dementia. This approach serves some goals well, such as increasing public awareness of the problem of Alzheimer's disease and generating funds for basic research. But a different strategy, forming coalitions with groups having similar aims, may have better long-term results. While there are important differences between dementia patients and others that are chronically ill, there are also important similarities. What happens to dementia patients and their families is only one example, albeit sometimes an extreme one, of a system of health care and social services that is poorly equipped to respond to chronic, disabling conditions.

Rather than focusing on a single disease, such as Alzheimer's disease, advocates may gather greater strength by working with like-minded advocates for other afflictions. One example is the Brain Damage Coalition of California, which brings together a diverse group of people who have similar legislative and policy concerns. Represented in the coalition are advocates for progressive brain diseases such as Alzheimer's disease, other dementias, Huntington's disease, Parkinson's disease, adult brain injury, and stroke.

The results of lobbying efforts are beginning to be seen. Legislative initiatives have been made in several states and at the federal level. Federal funding for research has increased dramatically. Several important pieces of legislation have been enacted in California which may dramatically alter the impact of dementia on the family. One bill creates ten regional centers throughout the state to coordinate services and provide information to families. Another has changed Medi-Cal (Medicaid) eligibility. Previously, if a patient was married, the couple had spend all their assets in order to qualify for Medi-Cal. This means that if the caregiver placed the patient in a nursing home, he must spend all the family's assets on institutional costs before the patient received Medi-Cal. The change allows an even division of the couple's estate, and the patient becomes eligible for Medi-Cal after his or her 50 percent is spent.

As the number of people living to old age increases, the incidence of all these forms of brain damage is rising. It is important to begin planning now to provide the supportive and health-related services that are needed. Although the initial cost will be high, changes in health policies will use available resources more appropriately to support home care, and can free family members from the staggering burdens they now have. For afflicted persons, as well as the rest of us who someday may develop brain damage, the development of a rational public policy for long-term care will mean that we do not have to fear becoming an overwhelming burden to our families, nor be treated in dehumanizing ways.

# REFERENCES

Albert, M. S., Geriatric neuropsychology, *Journal of Clinical and Consulting Psychology,* 1981, *49,* 835–850.

American Psychiatric Association, *Diagnostic and statistical manual of mental disorders.* 3rd ed., Washington, D.C., 1980.

Beck, A., D. Rush, D. Shaw, & G. Emery, *Cognitive therapy of depression.* New York: Guilford, 1979.

Blessed, G., B. E. Tomlinson, & M. Roth, The association between quantitative measures of dementia and of senile change in the cerebral gray matter of elderly subjects, *British Journal of Psychiatry,* 1968, *114,* 797–811.

Butler, R. N., & M. I. Lewis, *Aging and mental health,* 3rd ed. St. Louis: Mosby, 1982.

Cummings, J. L., & D. F. Benson, *Dementia: A clinical approach.* Boston: Butterworths, 1983.

Egan, G. *The Skilled helper.* Monterey, Calif.: Brooks/Cole Pub., 1975.

Eisdorfer, C., & D. Cohen, Diagnostic criteria for primary neuronal degeneration of the Alzheimer's type. Paper presented at the meetings of the Gerontological Society, Washington, D.C., 1979.

Folstein, J. F., S. E. Folstein, & P. R. McHugh, "Mini-mental state": A practical method for grading the cognitive state of patients for the clinician, *Journal of Psychiatric Research,* 1975, *12,* 189–198.

Funkenstein, H. H., R. Hicks, M. W. Dysken, & J. M. Davis, Drug treatment of cognitive impairment in Alzheimer's disease and the late life dementias. In N. E. Miller, & G. D. Cohen (eds.), *Clinical aspects of Alzheimer's disease and senile dementia.* New York: Raven, 1981.

Gallagher, D., & L. W. Thompson, Depression. In P. M. Lewinsohn, & L. Teri (eds.), *Clinical geropsychology: New directions in assessment and treatment.* New York: Pergamon, 1983.

Glasscote, R., J. E. Gudeman, & C. D. Miles, *Creative mental health services for the elderly.* Washington, D.C.: American Psychiatric Association, 1977.

## REFERENCES

Golden, C. J., T. A. Hammeke, & A. D. Purisch, Diagnostic validity of a standardized neuropsychological battery derived from Luria's neuropsychological test, *Journal of Consulting and Clinical Psychology*, 1978, *46*, 1258–1265.

Golden, C. J., et al., The Luria-Nebraska neuropsychological battery: Theoretical orientation and comment, *Journal of Consulting and Clinical Psychology*, 1982, *50*, 291–300.

Goldfried, M. R., & G. C. Davison, *Clinical behavior therapy*. New York: Holt, 1976.

Goodwin, J. S. & M. Regan, Cognitive dysfunction associated with naproxen and ibuprofen in the elderly, *Arthritis and Rheumatism*, 1982, *25*, 1013–1015.

Hachinski, V., N. Lassen, & J. Marshall, Multi-infarct dementia: A cause of mental deterioration in the elderly, *Lancet*, 1974, *2*, 207–210.

Hachinski, V. C., Differential diagnosis of Alzheimer's disease: Multi-infarct dementia. In B. Reisberg (ed.), Alzheimer's disease: The standard reference. New York: The Free Press, 1983.

Haley, J., *Problem-solving therapy*. San Francisco: Jossey-Bass, 1976.

Hartford, M. *Groups in social work*. New York: Columbia University Press, 1971.

Hassinger, M. J., J. M. Zarit, & S. H. Zarit, A comparison of clinical characteristics of multi-infarct and Alzheimer's dementia patients. Paper presented at the meetings of the Western Psychological Association, Sacramento, CA., 1982.

Heston, L. L. & J. A. White, *Dementia: A practical guide to Alzheimer's disease and related illnesses*. New York: W. H. Freeman, 1983.

Jacobs, J. W., M. R. Bernhard, A. Delgado, & J. J. Strain, Screening for organic mental syndromes in the medically ill, *Annals of Internal Medicine*, 1977, *86*, 40–46.

Jarvik, L. F., Genetic factors and chromosomal aberrations in Alzheimer's disease, senile dementia, and related disorders. In R. Katzman, R. D. Terry, & K. L. Bick (eds.), *Alzheimer's disease: Senile dementia and related disorders*. New York: Raven, 1978.

Kahn, R. L., The mental health system and the future aged, *Gerontologist*, 1975, *15*(1), 24–31.

Kahn, R. L., A. I. Goldfarb, M. Pollack, & R. Peck, Brief objective measures for the determination of mental status in the aged, *American Journal of Psychiatry*, 1960, *117*, 326–328.

Kahn, R. L., & N. E. Miller, Assessment of altered brain function in the aged. In M. Storandt, I. C. Siegler, & M. Elias (eds.), *The clinical psychology of aging*. New York: Plenum, 1978.

Kahn, R. L., S. H. Zarit, N. M. Hilbert, & G. Niederehe, Memory complaint and impairment in the aged, *Archives of General Psychiatry*, 1975, *32*, 1569–1573.

## REFERENCES

Katzman, R., Normal pressure hydrocephalus. In C. E. Wells (ed.), *Dementia, 2nd* ed. Philadelphia: Davis, 1977.

Lewinsohn, P. M., R. F. Munoz, M. A. Youngren, & A. M. Zeiss, *Control your depression.* Englewood Cliffs, N.J.: Prentice-Hall, 1978.

Lieberman, M. A., Yalom, I. D. & Miles, N. B. *Encounter groups: First facts.* New York: Basic Books, 1973.

Lipowski, Z. J., *Delirium.* Springfield, Ill.: Thomas, 1980.

Liston, E. H. & A. LaRue, Clinical differentiation of primary degenerative and multi-infarct dementia: A critical review of the evidence, part II, Pathological Studies, *Biological Psychiatry,* 1983, *12,* 1467–1483.

Lowenthal, M. F., P. Berkman, & Associates, *Aging and mental disorders in San Francisco.* San Francisco: Jossey-Bass, 1967.

Mace, N. L., & P. V. Rabins, *The 36-hour day.* Baltimore: Johns Hopkins University Press, 1981.

Matsuyama, H., Incidence of neurofibrillary changes, senile plaques, and granulovacuolar degeneration in aged individuals. In B. Reisberg (ed.), *Alzheimer's disease: The standard reference.* New York: The Free Press, 1983.

Mortimer, J. A., L. M. Schuman, & L. R. French, Epidemiology of dementing illness. In J. A. Mortimer, & L. M. Schuman (eds.), *The epidemiology of dementia.* New York: Oxford University Press, 1981.

Nandy, K., Immunologic factors. In B. Reisberg (ed.), *Alzheimer's disease: The standard reference.* New York: The Free Press, 1983.

NIA Task Force, Senility reconsidered, *Journal of the American Medical Association,* 1980, *244*(3), 259–263.

Orr, N. K., K. E. Reever, & S. H. Zarit, Longitudinal change in memory performance and self-report of memory problems. Paper presented at the meetings of the Gerontological Society. San Diego, Ca., 1980.

Perry, E. K. & R. H. Perry, Acetylcholinesterase in Alzheimer's disease. In B. Reisberg (ed.), *Alzheimer's disease: The standard reference.* New York: The Free Press, 1983.

Pfeiffer, E., A short portable mental status questionnaire for the assessment of organic brain deficit in elderly patients, *Journal of the American Geriatrics Society,* 1975, *23,* 433–439.

Popkin, S. J., D. Gallagher, L. W. Thompson, & M. Moore, Memory complaint and performance in normal and depressed older adults, *Experimental Aging Research,* 1982, *8,* 141–145.

Prinz, P. N., et al., Changes in the sleep and waking EEG in non-demented elderly, *Journal of the American Geriatrics Society,* 1982, 86–93.

Reisberg, B., *A guide to Alzheimer's disease.* New York: The Free Press, 1983.

Reisberg, B., S. H. Ferris, & T. Crook. Signs, symptoms, and course of age-associated cognitive decline. In S. Corkin, K. L. Davis, J. H. Growdon, E. Usdin, & R. J. Wurtman (eds), *Alzheimer's disease: A report*

**REFERENCES**

*of progress in research.* New York: Raven, 1982.

Rimm, D. C., & J. C. Masters, *Behavior therapy: Techniques and empirical findings.* 2nd ed., New York: Academic, 1978.

Rogers, C. R., *Client-centered therapy.* Boston: Houghton Mifflin, 1951.

Rosen, W. G., R. D. Terry, P. A. Fuld, R. Katzman, & A. Peck, Pathological verification of ischemic score in differentiation of dementias, *Annals of Neurology,* 1980, *7,* 486–488.

Rosenberg, G. S., B. Greenwald, & K. L. Davis, Pharmacologic treatment of Alzheimer's disease: An overview. In B. Reisberg (ed.), *Alzheimer's disease: The standard reference.* New York: The Free Press, 1983.

Roth, M., Senile dementia and its borderlands. In J. O. Cole, & J. E. Barrett (eds.), *Psychopathology in the aged.* New York: Raven, 1980.

Sabin, T. D., A. J. Vitug, & V. H. Mark, Are nursing home diagnosis and treatment adequate? *Journal of the American Medical Association,* 1982, *248,* 321–322.

Scheibel, A. B., Dendritic changes. In B. Reisberg (ed.), *Alzheimer's disease: The standard reference.* New York: Free Press, 1983.

Terry, R. D. Aging, senile dementia and Alzheimer's disease. In R. Katzman, R. D. Terry, & K. L. Bick (eds.), *Alzheimer's disease: Senile dementia and related disorders.* New York: Raven 1978.

Terry, R. D., & H. M. Wisniewski, Structural aspects of aging of the brain. In C. Eisdorfer, & R. O. Friedel (eds.), *Cognitive and emotional disturbance in the elderly.* Chicago: Year Book Medical Publishers, 1977.

Thompson, L. W., G. C. Davis, W. D. Obrist, & A. Heyman, Effects of hyperbaric oxygen on behavioral and physiological measures in elderly demented patients, *Journal of Gerontology,* 1976, *31,* 23–28.

Weinstein, E. A., & R. L. Kahn, *Denial of illness.* Springfield, Ill.: Thomas, 1955.

Yalom, I. D. *The theory and practice of group psychotherapy.* 2nd ed., New York: Basic Books, 1975.

Zarit, J., *Predictors of burden and distress for caregivers of dementia patients.* Unpublished doctoral dissertation, University of Southern California, 1982.

Zarit, S. H., *Aging and mental disorders: Psychological approaches to assessment and treatment.* New York: Free Press, 1980.

Zarit, S. H., Affective correlates of self-reports of memory, *International Journal of Behavioral Geriatrics,* 1982, *1,* 25–34.

Zarit, S. H., & C. R. Anthony, Interventions with dementia patients and their families. In J. E. Birren, M. Gilhooly and S. H. Zarit (eds.), *Alzheimer's disease: Policy and management.* Englewood-Cliffs, N.J.: Prentice-Hall, in press.

Zarit, S. H., J. Eiler, & M. J. Hassinger, Clinical assessment. In J. E. Birren, & K. W. Schaie (eds.), *Handbook of the psychology of aging.* 2nd

**REFERENCES**

ed., Englewood Cliffs, N.J.: Prentice-Hall, 1985.

Zarit, S. H., & R. L. Kahn, Impairment and adaptation in chronic disabilities, *Journal of Nervous and Mental Disease,* 1974, *159,* 63–72.

Zarit, S. H., N. E. Miller, & R. L. Kahn, Brain function, intellectual impairment and education in the aged, *Journal of the American Geriatrics Society,* 1978, *26,* 58–67.

Zarit, S. H., K. E. Reever, & J. Bach-Peterson, Relatives of the impaired elderly: Correlates of feelings of burden, *Gerontologist,* 1980, *20,* 649–655.

Zarit, S. H., J. M. Zarit, & K. E. Reever, Memory training for severe memory loss: Effects on senile dementia patients and their families, *Gerontologist,* 1982, *22,* 373–377.

# INDEX

# INDEX

Consequences, 101, 104
Counseling, individual, 4, 88, 89, 90, 113, 129, 134, 147
Creative Mental Health Programs for the Elderly, 195
CTscan (also CATscan), 41, 51
in Pick's disease, 17
in hydrocephalus, 20
Cummings, J.L., 12, 13, 15, 17, 18, 19

Daily records, 101–102, 107–108, 119, 127–128, 162, 164, 166, 171, 176, 194
Day care, 82, 97, 109, 110, 115, 127, 175, 176–177, 179–182
Delirium, 3, 10, 18, 19–24, 30–32, 34–35, 36, 37–40
definition, 30–32
described, 38, 55, 63–65
onset, 37–39, 42–43, 46, 51
Delusions, 19
Dementia, 29–67
causes, 9
definition, 9–10, 11, 30
described, 1–2, 27, 38, 52–56, 59–62
diagnostic criteria, 31, 38–40
history, 37–39, 41
onset, 37–39
overdiagnosis, 3, 15
progression, 38, 41
reversible, 9, 19–21, 42–43, 30, 140–141
Denial, 36, 38, 94, 122
Depression, 3, 9, 10, 24–26, 33, 36, 37–40, 46, 53, 58–59, 66–68
and caregiving, 61, 81, 182
and dementia, 25–26, 196
definition, 11, 21
described, 38, 66–68
onset, 37–39, 43
Disorientation, 19, 32–33, 125
Down's syndrome, 14
Drug-induced delirium, 23–24, 63, 140–141
Drug reactions, 20, 21, 23–24, 35–36, 42, 63, 125–126, 164, 185–193
Drugs, tranquilizing, 2, 6, 15, 24, 35, 185–194

Egan, G., 114, 117
Empathic listening, 114, 117, 123–124, 167, 170

Face-hand test, 39, 47–48, 56, 60, 66
Family meetings, 4, 88–90, 113, 131–146
followup, 141–142
process, 137–141
Focal brain damage, see Head trauma, Stroke

Gait disturbance, 20, 37
General anesthesia, 14, 22, 43
General paresis, 18, 19
Granulovacuolar structures, 12

Hachinski scoring system, 52, 53
Haldol (haloperidol), 35, 125–126, 164, 168, 187, 193
Haley, J., 114, 119
Hallucinations, 6, 19, 32, 38, 42, 55, 63–65, 79, 193
Hartford, M.E., 148
Head trauma, 3, 9, 14, 20, 24–25, 33, 36, 38–40, 43, 47, 206
definition, 11
mental status testing, 39, 47
Hereditability, 92
Heston, L. L., 92
Huntington's disease, 206
Hydrocephalus, 20, 22, 51

Illusions, 32, 34–35, 38, 79
Incontinence, 71, 75, 79, 165, 171–172
Insomnia, see Sleep disturbance

Jakob-Creutzfeld disease, 14, 18, 19

Kahn, R.L., 2, 29, 32
Kuru, 14, 18, 19

Language problems,
aphasia, 47, 31
in Pick's disease, 17
Lecithin, 92
Lewinsohn, P. M., 67, 119
Lewis, M. L., 36
Lieberman, M. A., 148

# INDEX